"This series of anecdotes . . . will probably help lift double-figure handicappers to greater heights on the course."

MX Brisbane, September 2010

"Great stories worthy of retelling at the 19th hole."

Sydney Morning Herald, 2011

"Eminently readable. It is a book that one can pick up and put down. However, when the time has come to put the book down, there is a strong urge to just read the next short chapter, and then the one after, and then . . . "

Golf Victoria and RMGC, December 2010

"An affectionately collated collection of anecdotes from the game's grand history . . . the real charm and effectiveness is in the sparse, elegant prose that recalls some of the great moments of the game and casts them in a refreshing new light."

Inside Sport, August 2010

"A charming collection . . . golfers will love this and anyone who has played sport will appreciate the life lessons from the links."

Alpha Magazine, October 2010

GOLF'S LIFE LESSONS

55 Inspirational Tales about Jack Nicklaus, Ben Hogan, Bobby Jones, and Others

Richard Allen

Foreword by Peter Thomson

Skyhorse Publishing

Skyhorse Publishing books may be purchased in bulk at special discounts for sales promotion, corporate gifts, fund-raising, or educational purposes. Special editions can also be created to specifications. For details, contact the Special Sales Department, Skyhorse Publishing, 307 West 36th Street, 11th Floor, New York, NY 10018 or info@skyhorsepublishing.com.

Skyhorse® and Skyhorse Publishing® are registered trademarks of Skyhorse Publishing, Inc.®, a Delaware corporation.

Visit our website at www.skyhorsepublishing.com.

10 9 8 7 6 5 4

Library of Congress Cataloging-in-Publication Data is available on file.

Design and typography © Melbourne University Publishing

Text design by Designland
Typeset by Mike Kuszla

Cover design by Qualcom Designs
Cover photo credit: Associated Press

ISBN: 978-1-5107-4071-6
Ebook ISBN 978-1-5107-4072-3

Printed in the United States of America

To Richard Stanley Allen,

who always played the game in the right spirit.

Foreword

The game of golf is essentially a solitary sport. A golfer hits his own ball exclusively and counts his own score. Yet, at the same time, it is social intercourse where souls of like mind mingle, chasing after the same goal.

It has been so for 600 years in various forms, yet it comes to us now as a world leisure pursuit, enjoyed by some thirty million players, with more populations attracted to it each passing year. Why has it such a draw across so many countries and so many climates? The answer is kept in the essence of the game itself: it mirrors human behavior, and this remarkable book aims to prove it.

In the beginning, golf was played over "links" such as St. Andrews by—it was said—all and sundry. They even formed themselves into societies convened to pass rules of play and etiquette. Mary, Queen of Scots, was introduced to the game in St. Andrews in the mid-1500s. It was not a royal game until much later, but gradually affluence allowed the wealthy to pursue it. To this day, it seems the sport of the affluent.

In time it became an industry, because balls had to be manufactured and implements had to be created by hand. At the same time, tutors of the game emerged to help the unskilled and generally demonstrate the art of the game. Strangely, championships were not arranged until 1754, when the Society of St. Andrews Golfers chased a silver-plated club, donated by an elite group of individuals, bent on the purpose of boosting the standing of the game over the Links. The first winner was a merchant from the town, and for his troubles he was immediately elected captain of the club for the ensuing year, an act that is perpetuated to this very day, although club captains are no longer deemed the best players.

Championships have become largely events for professional players, who become idols of the sport. Their mechanical movements and their mental approaches are served up to an enquiring multitude, who search for the game's secrets. It is this delving that is so fascinating. Thoughts on the playing of golf come in streams of psychotherapeutics for the mystified.

Yet the subject of "thoughts on golf" boils down to common sense, allowing for decision making of simple proportions and a twist of gumption. Alas, we golfers are still at the mercy of our own selves, strong of mind when the going is good, but pathetically weak when pressure exerts. Isn't that life itself?

One famous medico, who thought he knew most of the inner secrets of players at large, prescribed the playing of golf as a sure cure for bolshevism. He may have been right. Golf was branded an antirevolutionary pastime in the communist countries until they fell apart.

Golf may have saved them.

Peter Thomson

Contents

Introduction

·············•·············

Golf is both deceptively simple and endlessly complex. It is humbling, gratifying, maddening, and unfair. This is why there is no better sporting metaphor for life.

Golf requires honesty and humility, persistence and patience, tenacity and self-belief. It teaches respect, modesty, and perspective. It celebrates courage and exposes greed. It demands that self-doubt and disappointment be faced.

Billy Casper, one of the world's greatest putters, said golf "puts a man's character to the anvil and his richest qualities—patience, poise, restraint—to the flame."

Golf can be both capricious and cruel, so it promotes dignity and good grace. "Golfers are great losers," said former professional David Feherty. "The world's number one tennis player spends 90 percent of his time winning, while the world's number one golfer spends 90 percent of his time losing."

Golf requires constant decision-making. It necessitates the continual weighing up of risk and reward. It is unpredictable, so it teaches us—as Kipling implores—to meet with triumph and disaster. Crucially, the more we play golf, the more we realize that we should not take the game—or life—too seriously.

When played competitively, golf is a game that relentlessly examines the soul. Hale Irwin, winner of three U.S. Opens, said, "The longer you play, the more certain you are that a man's performance is the outward manifestation of who, in his heart, he really thinks he is."

The great Bobby Jones—the only person ever to have won the U.S. Open, U.S. Amateur, British Open, and British Amateur in the same year—had a similar take on it: "I had held a notion that I could make a pretty fair appraisal of the worth of an opponent simply by speaking to him on the first tee and taking a good measuring look into his eyes."

Golf, probably the world's most civilized game, breeds manners and honesty: count your strokes, penalize yourself, play the ball where it lies, accept bad luck, rake bunkers, repair pitch marks, fill in divots, keep quiet while others play, tend the flag.

Conceptually, golf is easy: hit a stationary ball into eighteen separate holes, each one 4.3 inches in diameter, with asymmetric implements over a route of more than 3.7 miles.

The complications are many. Trees, bunkers, and rough can impede progress. Wind makes balls do strange things in the air. On the green, there are humps and swales to deal with.

The golf swing, which uses sixty-four major muscles and 230 individual movements, causes its own problems. It can cause shanks, smothers, tops, slices, hooks, pulls, skies, and, occasionally, air shots. Golf, then, becomes a cerebral exercise: assess the dangers, quantify your skills, and minimize the damage, with the aim of taking the lowest number of strokes on each hole.

Golf doesn't care how you get the ball in the hole. "It's not called pretty, it's called golf," Claude Harmon, 1948 Masters winner, used to tell his students. A 70-year-old who hits the ball 197 yards off the tee can whip a 17-year-old who hits it 273 yards. And both of them know it.

Golf is a great leveler. The game does not care who you

are, what you have, or whom you know. And it can be played forever. In 2007, Canadian Ed Ervasti, at age ninety-three, shot 72 at the Sunningdale Golf and Country Club in London, Ontario, breaking his age by 21 strokes.

Importantly, golf breeds empathy. No fans better understand the professionals in their chosen sport as much as golfers do. When a professional golfer fluffs a shot, spectators don't laugh, they feel pain, because they have faced the same challenges and been found equally wanting. A delicate chip over a bunker from a tight lie is a tough shot, no matter who you are.

To see great golfers at work, and to witness how they approach the demands of their chosen craft, is to witness life's challenges writ small.

"I'm not going to get it close, I'm going to make it," said Tom Watson to his caddie as he stood over his ball in heavy rough on the seventeenth hole at Pebble Beach in the 1982 U.S. Open. And he made it. And why shouldn't he believe he would? He had practiced the shot for hours leading up to the tournament.

Tiger Woods's 15-shot win in the same tournament and venue in 2000 was a demonstration of supreme focus and single-mindedness. Mid-tournament, Denmark's Thomas

Bjorn said that Woods was "playing every shot like his life depends on it." Irishman Padraig Harrington said at the completion of the tournament, "I looked at the scoreboard in total wonderment."

Greg Norman's statement after blowing the play-off for the 1989 British Open at Royal Troon is a life lesson for golfers and nongolfers alike: "Destiny has a funny way of saying, 'Hey, this is how it's going to be.' But we all accept fate. It's what keeps us coming back, hoping. You have got to think positively."

Jack Nicklaus's dramatic win in the 1986 Masters, aged forty-six, showed how the naysayers could be proven wrong, while Hale Irwin's grinding win in the 1974 U.S. Open at Winged Foot was a demonstration of gimlet-eyed, never-say-die doggedness. And who could forget the courage shown by Ben Hogan when he won the 1950 U.S. Open at Merion less than seventeen months after nearly dying in a horrific car crash?

The unheralded Johnny Goodman was an example of quiet determination in the face of extreme odds when he beat Bobby Jones in the first round of the 1929 U.S. Amateur. Everyone on the planet (except perhaps Goodman himself) thought he would be cannon fodder for the world's best player.

Twenty-five years earlier, 42-year-old Walter Travis, originally from Australia, became the first non-Brit to win the British Amateur, despite the fact that his opponent in the final constantly outdrove him by 55 yards. Amazingly, Travis—who also won three U.S. Amateur titles—did not pick up a golf club until he was thirty-four.

Bobby Jones calling a penalty on himself for a moving ball during the 1925 U.S. Open at the Worcester Country Club in Massachusetts, a tournament he eventually lost by a shot, was a demonstration of supreme honesty. No one else saw his ball move. Jones refused to accept praise for his actions. The glorious thing is that thousands of golfers around the world make similar confessions every day.

Most important, golf breeds friendship. Golfers are not bonded together, they are welded. The expression "Where would you rather be?" is surely uttered more often on golf courses than at any other place. Golfers belong to an exclusive club, joined together by the joy and spirit of their game.

Confidence

............●............

*I never wanted to be a millionaire. I just wanted
to live like one.*

WALTER HAGEN

*Golf never had a showman like Hagen. All the professionals who
have a chance to go after big money today should say a silent thanks
to Walter each time they stretch a cheque between their fingers.*

GENE SARAZEN, *THIRTY YEARS OF CHAMPIONSHIP GOLF*

In April 1928, American professional Walter Hagen arrived in
England for the British Open, which was to be held at Royal

1

St. George's on the Kent coast. His appearance caused quite a stir. Touring professionals were rare, especially professionals as unusual as Hagen. Locals were intrigued by his swing—a wide stance, strong grip, flat swing plane, and lurching follow-through, probably the legacy of Hagen's first sporting love, baseball.

They also whispered among themselves about Hagen's flashy car and dandy clothes. He liked to play in plus-fours made from alpaca wool, a bow tie, and a white shirt with gold cufflinks. You could see the part in his brilliantined hair from 100 yards away (he would eventually be sponsored by Brylcreem). And he always played with a smile.

Hagen's manager, Bob Harlow, never one to pass up an opportunity to generate interest in his player—nor some extra winnings—had arranged for Hagen to play a series of exhibition matches during his visit. One was a 72-hole match at Moor Park, near London, against the British Ryder Cup player Archie Compston, with the winner getting £500. Hagen—not long off the boat, where he had prepared assiduously with late-night drinking sessions—lost by the staggering margin of 18 down with 17 to play. There was an accusation that he played "frivolous" golf. Regardless, it was a monumental drubbing, especially for a professional who had won two U.S. Opens.

After the match, Hagen posed for pictures, smiling his broadest smile and chatting happily to the press. He then left in his car with Harlow. A long, very pointed silence ensued, which was broken by Hagen: "What's the matter with you? You're not worried about that, are you? I can beat that sonofabitch the best day he ever had." A week later, Hagen won his third British Open at Royal St. George's, shooting 292; Compston came third.

Hagen was a natural. Over the course of his career, in addition to two U.S. Opens—he won his first in 1914 at only his second appearance in the tournament—he won five U.S. Professional Golfers' Association (PGA) championships. He also won four British Opens in a remarkable eight-year stretch and was generally recognized as golf's first millionaire.

During the summer of 1924, after he had won his second British Open at Royal Liverpool, the *New York Times* described Hagen as "the greatest golfer who ever lived—bar none." His secret, in addition to a short game that got him out of countless jams, was an unwavering confidence in his own ability.

In the 1925 PGA championship at Olympia Fields in Illinois, Hagen famously walked into the locker room and asked Leo Diegel and Al Watrous, "Which one of you is going to finish second?" He polished off Watrous in the first round and Diegel in the third.

During his last British Open win in 1929 at Muirfield in Scotland, he shot 67 in the second round—at the time, it was the lowest round ever recorded in championship golf. With two rounds to go, he was two strokes behind Diegel. Late in the night before the 36-hole final day, Hagen was holding court, whiskey in hand. Someone pointed out that perhaps he should think about retiring, given that Diegel had gone to bed hours beforehand. "Yeah," Hagen retorted, "but he ain't sleeping."

On the first tee the next day, in a gale, Hagen brought out a mallet-headed, deep-faced driver. He hit his ball no more than 7 yards off the ground for the next thirty-six holes, shooting a pair of 75s and winning by six shots. Diegel shot 82, then 77.

Henry Longhurst recounted a story about Hagen at another British Open, at Carnoustie in 1937. Longhurst was sitting in the bar at half-past one in the morning: "In walked Hagen with a basket under his arm. In it were half a dozen trout. He was lying well up the championship, but that had not stopped him driving 70 miles for an evening's fishing. He took the fish down to the kitchen, gutted them, and solemnly cooked them for his supper."

Hagen displayed the same confidence with women as he did with his golfing opponents. He reportedly once looked at the ample bosom of the Metropolitan Opera singer Ernestine Schumann-Heink and said, "My dear, did you ever stop to think what a lovely bunker you would make?" Hagen was twice married and divorced, at a time when divorce was rare.

He was also a generous man who never forgot his own modest upbringing. He gave away large sums of money to his friends and to caddies—one of whom famously received Hagen's 1922 British Open winner's check for £50—and played in many exhibition matches for charity.

But confidence was his dominant trait. In 1924, during the British Open at Royal Liverpool, Hagen frittered away shots on the first nine holes of the final round and had to play the last nine in par to match Ernest Whitcombe's total of 302. He holed several improbable putts and got up and down from greenside bunkers on three occasions. With two holes to go, Hagen led by

5

one. He parred the seventeenth and lay 10 feet away for three on the last, with one putt to win. Most golfers would have studied the putt for a considerable time, but Hagen strolled up, scarcely took aim, and rapped it in.

Someone commented to Hagen later that he seemed to take the last putt very casually and asked if he knew he had to make it for the win. Hagen's response was that, in fact, he considered he had two shots to win. "No man ever beat *me* in a play-off," he said.

When Hagen died in 1969, the pastor at his funeral, Edwin Shroeder, finished the service with the words, "His biggest game is over. He putted out."

Focus

...............•...............

Ben Hogan is what is known as a hard case. You could see him sitting
at a poker table saying, "Your thousand—and another five." He
might have four aces, or a pair of twos.

HENRY LONGHURST, *A HARD CASE FROM TEXAS*

Hogan gave away less about himself than any
man I ever met.

SAM SNEAD

At the 1947 Masters at Augusta National in Georgia, Claude
Harmon and Ben Hogan stood on the tee of the fearsome

par-three twelfth hole, described by Lloyd Mangrum as the "meanest little hole in the world." Although only 153 yards long, making it the shortest hole at Augusta, it boasts a creek in front of the green and three carefully postioned greenside bunkers—one short and two long—which make distance control crucial.

Hogan, away first, squinted at the treetops, judging the wind strength and direction, before selecting his club. He chose well, his ball flying high and straight and landing a yard beyond the hole. Harmon's ball flew equally high, and equally straight, arcing over Rae's Creek and rattling into the cup for a hole in one. The crowd whooped. Harmon jumped in the air, shook his caddie's hand, and waved his hat.

The two players walked across the bridge over Rae's Creek. Harmon trotted over to the hole and picked out his ball, again to the crowd's acclamation. Then Hogan lined up his putt and holed it.

Hogan had so far said nothing about the hole in one, which puzzled Harmon. Then, as the men walked onto the thirteenth tee, Hogan finally said, "You know, Claude, you might find this hard to believe, but in all the years I've been playing The Masters, that's the first time I've birdied the twelfth."

You're Never Too Young

...........●...........

Tiger told me later that he remembers hitting only one "perfect" golf

shot in 2000, a year where he won

12 times around the world. It was a three-wood on

the fourteenth hole of the Old Course during the

Open Championship.

CLAUDE "BUTCH" HARMON, *THE PRO*

The bigger the event, the higher he'll raise the bar. He's Michael

Jordan in long pants.

PAUL AZINGER AT THE 1997 MASTERS

His swing was too fast, his drives too erratic. His short game was not sharp enough, his putting was too streaky. He was, simply, too *young*.

Much was said about 21-year-old Tiger Woods—a mixed-race, middle-class kid who learned his golf on municipal courses in Los Angeles—as he prepared to play as a professional for the first time at The Masters in Augusta, Georgia, in 1997, eight months after turning pro.

Woods's two previous appearances at The Masters, as an amateur, had resulted in an equal forty-first placing and a missed cut—hardly the stuff of a would-be champion. Sure, he had had a stellar amateur career, including three U.S. Amateur Championship titles. But, said the naysayers, great amateurs who can't cut it in professional ranks are a dime a dozen. The pundits said he would be overawed, that Magnolia Lane would choke him. He would wilt under the blowtorch applied by his hard-bitten, experienced colleagues.

Woods didn't listen to any of this. In the lead-up to the tournament, he was too busy practicing golf and playing computer games with a buddy in his rented Augusta house.

Nine holes into his opening round, Woods had shot a four-over-par 40, and the sceptics had only grown in number.

Never before, they trumpeted to anyone who would listen, had anyone shot 40 on the first nine of The Masters and won the tournament. But this would be no ordinary Masters. Woods birdied the tenth, twelfth, and thirteenth, eagled the fifteenth, and then birdied the seventeenth. A back nine of 30 gave him a very respectable first-round score of 70.

From then on, the tournament became the Tiger show. Woods shot 66 in the second round and at the halfway mark was 20 shots ahead of Nick Faldo, the previous year's winner. On the Saturday, he shot 65 and increased his lead from three shots to nine. Paul Stankowski, ten behind with a round to go, spoke for everyone when he said, "I might have a chance if I make five or six birdies in the first two or three holes."

Woods rounded things off with a 69 in the final round for a total of 270, and the records toppled. His eighteen under par total was the lowest score in the tournament's history, one better than the 271 shot by Jack Nicklaus thirty-two years earlier. He won by an outlandish 12 shots, three more than the previous winning margin, again achieved by Nicklaus. The only person who had ever bettered this winning margin in a major was Old Tom Morris at the 1862 British Open.

Far from being erratic, Woods's drives proved his most

11

effective weapon. The longest club he hit into a par four all week was a seven-iron. Extraordinarily, on the Thursday and Friday, he hit a wedge into the 492-yard par-five fifteenth hole. For his second shot, that is. His average drive that week was a shade under 328 yards, more than 22 yards longer than his closest rival.

And the young Woods's putting wasn't too shabby, either: he did not three-putt once all week.

You're Never Too Old

.... ● ....

You seem to forget that luck is a part of the game and a good golfer must be good at all parts of the game.

WALTER TRAVIS, WHEN IT WAS SUGGESTED TO HIM THAT HE LOST THE
U.S. AMATEUR BECAUSE OF AN OPPONENT'S GOOD LUCK

Travis holed out from such immeasurable distances that his opponents claimed he could putt the eyes out of a chipmunk.

CHARLES PRICE, *GOLFER-AT-LARGE*

Walter Travis grew up in the small Australian town of Maldon in the Victorian Goldfields, the fourth of 11 children. When he left for America in 1886 at the age of twenty-three to represent construction product exporters McLean Brothers and Rigg, he could never have envisaged the extraordinary future he would have in golf.

In fact, when he left Australia's shores, Travis had likely never heard of the game. But he was certainly aware of it by 1895, when a golf course was slated for Flushing, New York, where he had moved five years earlier. Travis thought the idea laughable—golf, after all, was still a mystery outside Britain, and he couldn't see what all the fuss was about—but not wanting to be left out, he bought a set of clubs anyway. He first hit a ball in October 1896 at the Oakland Golf Club on Long Island, three months before his thirty-fifth birthday.

He later wrote about how he became "an infatuated devotee" of the game, poring over instruction books by Horace Hutchinson and Willie Park, devising practice drills, tinkering with both his swing and his clubs, and trying out new ball types. He became an addict and practiced for hours on end. Within a year, he had won the championship at Oakland Golf

14

Club, scoring 82. It was an impressive feat, but bigger things awaited.

The following year—1898—Travis entered his first U.S. Amateur Championship at Morris County Golf Club in New York, losing in the semifinal to Findlay Douglas, who went on to win the championship. Travis's fellow competitors saddled him with a nickname, The Old Man, because of his advanced years. This did nothing but spur him to better things.

Travis's loss to Douglas drove him to practice even harder, and two years later, only four years after he had first picked up a club, he won the U.S. Amateur Championship at Garden City, New York, beating his nemesis Findlay Douglas, 2 up. And he did it while experimenting with a new type of ball, the Haskell rubber-core. He won the same event the following year at the Country Club of Atlantic City, in New Jersey, and then again two years later at the Nassau Country Club on Long Island. He also came equal second in the 1902 U.S. Open at Garden City.

By this stage, Travis was clearly the country's top amateur golfer. But never one for shirking a challenge, in 1904, at the age of forty-two, Travis traveled to Royal St. George's on the Kent coast in England to compete alongside 103 other competitors

15

in the British Amateur Championship. After accounting for former champions Horace Hutchinson and Harold Hilton, as well as two-time finalist James Robb, Travis met Edward Blackwell in the final.

Blackwell was a big hitter—he consistently outdrove Travis by 55 yards—but Travis, using a new center-shafted putter, more than made up for this on the greens, holing several putts of 49 feet or more. He defeated Blackwell 4 and 3 to become the first non-Brit to win the championship.

History says that Travis was not welcomed warmly by his English hosts, no doubt largely because of his gruff demeanor on the course. Travis always maintained he needed the utmost silence on the course to help him concentrate and had no time for small talk. He also followed the rules of the game with a fanatical obstinacy and insisted his playing partners do the same. If this didn't win him friends, it at least won him a grudging respect. But nonetheless, after Travis had won, the captain of St. George's, Lord Northbourne, began his speech: "Not since the days of Caesar has the British nation been subjected to such a humiliation." Travis left the UK the next day, the British Amateur trophy firmly tucked under his arm, and never returned.

It was to be another 22 years before another non-Brit, Jess Sweetser of the Siwanoy Club in New York, would win the British Amateur Championship, despite the fact that many great American golfers attempted it, including Jerome Travers, Francis Ouimet, and Bobby Jones.

Ironically, for a man who was initially skeptical of the future of the game of golf in the United States, Travis did more for its popularity there than perhaps anyone who preceded him. When he won the British Amateur, interest in golf surged throughout his adopted country.

Travis remained a steely competitor into his fifties. Aged fifty-three, he lost the semifinal of the 1914 U.S. Amateur at Ekwanok Country Club in Vermont to 27-year-old Travers. The following year, he sank a 33-foot putt on the final hole to vanquish Travers and win his fourth Metropolitan Golf Association Championship.

Throughout his playing career, Travis also wrote about his passion. In 1901, he published *Practical Golf*, closely followed by *The Art of Putting*, and in 1908, he began publishing *American Golfer* magazine. As if that weren't enough, he was also closely involved in the design and construction of more than 40 golf courses, including such notables as Pine Valley and Pinehurst No. 2.

Entirely self-taught, Travis achieved success in golf on both sides of the Atlantic through determination, dedication, hard work, and an absolute unwillingness to believe that he was too old to compete at the highest level.

Amateurism

............•............

In the 1920s amateur golf was still regarded as the higher calling. As far as golf's establishment was concerned the professional game was a cheap carnival and its practitioners a sideshow attraction. Amateurs played for love; professionals bore the stigma of commerce. The amateur played with a certain careless grace, never committing the cardinal sin of wanting to win too much.

MICHAEL BLAINE, *THE KING OF SWINGS*

A completely charming person without any semblance of aggressiveness on the golf course.

BOBBY JONES ON FELLOW AMATEUR ROGER WETHERED

The 1921 British Open, held on the Old Course at St. Andrews in Scotland, had a most unusual finish, one that highlights the differences between the game back then, in which amateurs played a significant part, and today's highly professional game.

At the end of four rounds, two players were tied at 296 strokes. One was a gnarly professional, Jock Hutchison, a native of St. Andrews who, twenty years earlier, had left Scotland to seek fame and fortune in the United States and was living in Chicago. The other was 20-year-old Roger Wethered, a fresh-faced amateur from Surrey in England, brother of the well-known female golfer Joyce Wethered, of whom Bobby Jones once said, "I have not played golf with anyone, man or woman, amateur or professional, who made me feel so utterly outclassed."

Neither Hutchison nor Wethered had completed the four rounds without incident. Wethered had incurred a penalty stroke in the third round for treading on his ball, while Hutchison had had a hole in one on the eighth hole in the first round and came within a few inches of another hole in one on the very next hole, a short par four.

After the fourth-round scores had been checked, the tournament organizers, the Royal and Ancient Golf Club of

St. Andrews, confirmed that the players were tied and told them there would be a 36-hole play-off the next day. Wethered informed them, very politely, that he was unable to take part in this play-off, as he had committed to playing in an English village cricket match and ought to be making tracks to the railway station to catch the next southbound train. He congratulated Hutchison on his fine and well-deserved victory and went to collect his belongings.

The reaction of the officials can only be imagined. Here was a golfer refusing to play off for the oldest and greatest championship in the land because of a cricket match . . . in England!

Were it not for a group of Wethered's friends, who had come to watch him in the final round, he most probably would have boarded the train. They cajoled him into staying and completing the task. Surely, they pointed out, his cricket team could enlist the help of someone else just this once.

Eventually, Wethered relented. He lost the play-off the next day by nine shots, shooting 159 to Hutchison's 150. History didn't record the result of the Wethered-less cricket match.

Seizing the Moment

·············•·············

Kill.

CADDIE JEFF 'SQUEAKY' MEDLEN TO JOHN DALY ON

EACH TEE OF THE 1991 U.S. PGA, CROOKED STICK

GOLF CLUB, INDIANA

I don't even drive that far when I go on vacation.

RAYMOND FLOYD, ON JOHN DALY'S LONG GAME

In 1991, a relative newcomer to the US tour, 25-year-old Californian John Daly, dreamed of playing in his first U.S. PGA championship, to be held at Crooked Stick Golf Club in

Carmel, Indiana, a suburb of Indianapolis. There was one major problem: he hadn't qualified. As the tournament date approached, he was ninth alternate—meaning nine people would have to drop out of the field for him to get entry.

The week before the tournament, Daly missed the cut in the Buick Open in Grand Blanc, Michigan. Disappointed, he drove more than 930 miles south to his home in Arkansas. He had no plans for the subsequent week. Then the following happened.

Japanese player Jumbo Ozaki and American Paul Azinger pulled out of the PGA field with injuries. Australian Rodger Davis decided to play in Europe. Irishman Ronan Rafferty withdrew because he and his wife were expecting a baby. Crooked Stick head professional Jim Ferriel decided not to play so that he could concentrate on merchandising opportunities at the tournament. Englishman Mark James withdrew so he could concentrate on winning Ryder Cup points in Europe. Gibby Gilbert and Lee Trevino both pulled out. Marco Dawson shot 74 in the final round of the Buick Open and finished tenth, which lost him his spot in the PGA field.

Daly had been keeping a close eye on this chain of events, and at five o'clock on the day before the tournament was due to start, he set off on the seven-hour drive to Indianapolis, despite the fact that he still was not officially in the field. Waiting for him at his hotel was a message from the PGA informing him that he was playing.

Crooked Stick had been lengthened to more than 7,200 yards, making it the second-longest in PGA history. After three practice rounds, Jack Nicklaus had labeled it the most difficult course he had ever played. Daly had not had the luxury of a practice round.

On the first day, as two-time U.S. Open champion Curtis Strange shot 81 and left the course in a huff, Daly shot 69, using his oversize driver to pulverize the ball, hitting it to parts of the course that experts had thought it was not possible to reach. Bruce Lietzke later said, "The first two or three drives he hit I wasn't able to see, because the ball came off the club face faster than I was used to."

Two weeks beforehand, Cobra sales representative Arnie Cunningham, having heard that Daly's drivers kept breaking, gave him an Ultramid driver to try. The driver's head was made from a thermoplastic used by German police for their riot vests.

People expected that Daly's strength—his ability to hit the ball prodigious distances (his nickname was "Wild

Thing")—would eventually be his undoing. Although he was ranked first in driving distance on the tour, he was 185th in driving accuracy. But he silenced the doubters by shooting 67 in the second round and then birdied the eighteenth for a third-round 69, giving him a three-shot lead with a round to go.

On the final day, he birdied the second, fifth, thirteenth, and fifteenth holes and recorded his only major blemish on the seventeenth—a double bogey—by which time the tournament was over. He shot 71 and won by three shots. Over the course of the tournament, Daly had hit 35 of 56 fairways and 54 of 72 greens and had putted out of his mind.

The crowd took Daly into their hearts, partly because of his Cinderella-like entry into the tournament and partly because of his go-for-broke approach. And his refreshing answers to media questions were a writer's dream. When it was suggested to him that there was something magical about his driver, he replied, "A friend of mine took a .44 magnum and blew the head off [the driver], so they're not bulletproof."

Refusing to Be Overawed

..............•..............

Anything can happen in golf. Anybody can beat anybody on any given day. If that weren't the case, there'd be no reason to play.

CLAUDE HARMON, *THE PRO*

This game is great and very strange.

SEVE BALLESTEROS

Johnny Goodman, an orphan from Omaha, Nebraska, learned the game of golf in the 1920s just like many of the less well-off did—by caddying. It was said that Goodman hit his short irons so straight that, when walking from his home to the Field Club, he would hit wedges along the Union Pacific railway track, keeping his ball inside the rails the whole way.

In 1929, at the height of Bobby Jones's dominance, Goodman, aged nineteen, rode the train third class to Pebble Beach in California to play in the U.S. Amateur Championship. As bad luck would have it, he was drawn to play Jones, his hero, in the first match-play round. Jones had won four of the previous five U.S. Amateur titles and was the short-price favorite, and thousands gathered at Pebble Beach to witness the slaughter. The night before the match, Goodman's mentor, Bert Waddington, refused to tell his teenage charge whom he had been drawn to play, for fear that his player wouldn't sleep.

The next day, Goodman was, remarkably, 1 up after nine holes. The spectators were convinced that Jones would hit his straps on the second nine, as he always did. But Jones's famous putter, Calamity Jane, went awry, and Goodman still led by one as the players walked to the last tee. They both posted fives on the eighteenth, Jones's second shot bouncing off a tree to land back in the middle of the fairway, from where he failed to get up and down.

Goodman had beaten the best golfer in the world. Fans were shocked and then became angry that Goodman had had the temerity to beat Jones, whom many clearly considered had a divine right to win the tournament. The *New York Times* called Jones's defeat "nothing short of a calamity." One journalist wrote, "If you're giving a show, don't kill the star in the prologue."

Many spectators left for home once Jones was out of the tournament, and the gate receipts fell accordingly. The tournament was a fizzer, despite the fact that it finished in spectacular circumstances. On the last hole of the final, Harrison Johnston hit his ball onto the beach, where he found it being washed in and out by the waves. He calmly waited for the waves to recede, pulled off a miraculous recovery shot, parred the hole, and won the event.

The Jones/Goodman issue festered for a long time, largely because Goodman, as a young ex-caddie, did not come from the so-called "right side of the tracks." It would take five years for Goodman to be treated fairly by the United States Golf Association and awarded a spot in the Walker Cup team—the amateur teams match between the United States and Britain. In the meantime, Goodman would win the 1933 U.S. Open at North Shore, Illinois, and later the 1937 U.S. Amateur in Portland, Oregon.

Johnny Goodman remains the last amateur to win the U.S. Open.

Setting Records

...........•...........

Afterwards I looked at the scoreboard in total wonderment.

IRISHMAN PADRAIG HARRINGTON AT THE COMPLETION OF THE 2000

U.S. OPEN

*In the last two years he has refined his game, and now he is the
world's best driver of the ball, its best iron player, best chipper and
best putter. But above all he is the game's most focused player.*

JOHN GARRITY, *SPORTS ILLUSTRATED*, JUNE 2000, ON TIGER WOODS

As dusk was drawing in on the eve of the 2000 U.S. Open
at Pebble Beach, California, a lonely figure could be seen

tinkering around on the practice green. On the face of it, the player needn't have been there at all. He had won eleven of his previous twenty PGA Tour starts and had just spent three solid days at Las Vegas with his coach refining an already very refined swing.

The following day, after his opening round of 65—including a miserly twenty-four putts—had cut through the field like a cleaver, Tiger Woods explained his extended putting practice the night before.

"I didn't like the way I was rolling the ball. I was making quite a few putts in practice rounds, but the ball wasn't turning over the way I would like to see it roll. I worked on it for a couple of hours and found that my posture was a little off. My release wasn't quite right," he said.

Until then, some of the other players in the field might not have known what they were up against in this, the millennial Open.

Denmark's Thomas Bjorn later succinctly summed up Woods's approach: "He's playing every shot like his life depends on it."

Woods's opening round gave him a one-stroke lead in a day when only ten players broke 70. A second-round 69 took his lead to six strokes, and a third-round 71—in difficult winds, and which included a triple bogey—extended his lead to ten.

During the final round, Woods parred the first nine holes, then birdied the tenth, twelfth, thirteenth, and fourteenth to shoot 67. Notably, he concentrated just as much on his final shot—a 1-yard, uphill, right-to-left putt—as he did on his opening drive. He made the putt, of course, held up his right fist, and flashed a grin that lit up Carmel.

Woods finished twelve under par and was the only player in red figures. Runners-up Ernie Els and Miguel Angel Jimenez finished at three over par. His winning margin eclipsed, by two shots, the previous greatest winning margin in a major, set by Old Tom Morris at the 1862 British Open at Prestwick, in a field of twelve players.

During the week, Woods made just five bogies and did not have a single three-putt green. In seventy-two holes, he required only 110 putts and made par-saving putts seemingly from everywhere.

By the time he holed out on Sunday afternoon, Woods had created or matched several tournament records—the largest margin of victory (fifteen strokes), the lowest 72-hole score (272, tied with Jack Nicklaus and Lee Janzen), the largest lead

31

after thirty-six and fifty-four holes, the lowest 36-hole score (134, tied with Nicklaus, T.C. Chen, and Janzen), and the most strokes under par (twelve, tied with Gil Morgan, who reached that mark in the third round in 1992 at Pebble Beach, before finishing thirteenth).

"We always felt someone would come along who could drive the ball 300 yards and putt like Ben Crenshaw," said Nick Price after the tournament finished. "This guy drives the ball farther than anybody I've ever seen and putts better than Crenshaw. He's a phenomenon."

Woods said after the final round that his game plan was deceptively simple: "Today I wanted to go out there and make absolutely no bogeys. I just felt that if I could keep grinding, keep grinding and stick to doing what I was doing all week, which was hitting fairways. If I had a good situation, attack . . . And concentrate on those big par putts because I knew I was going to have one or two here and there, and I made all of them."

In 2000, Woods would win nine PGA Tour titles. At the end of the year, he led the tour in 22 statistical categories, including a scoring average of 67.79, the lowest in history.

Honesty

..............•..............

*Golf is like solitaire. When you cheat, you cheat
only yourself.*

TONY LEMA

*Golfers should not fail to realize that it is a game of great traditions,
of high ideals of sportsmanship, one in which
a strict adherence to the rules is essential.*

FRANCIS OUIMET

The raging favorite at the 1925 U.S. Open Championship at the Worcester Country Club in Massachusetts was amateur golfer Bobby Jones. He had won the U.S. Open two years earlier at New York's Inwood Country Club, as well as the 1924 U.S. Amateur Championship at the Merion Golf Club in Philadelphia.

During the 1925 championship, Jones found his ball sitting in long grass on a steep bank by the eleventh green. He took his stance and was about to hit the ball when it moved. Jones immediately alerted the nearby marshals. However, they said that they had seen nothing, and neither had the spectators who were standing close by. The marshals put the onus back on Jones, who insisted on taking a one-shot penalty.

Although he could not have known at the time, his actions, though applauded, would eventually lose him the tournament. After four rounds, he was tied with Willie Macfarlane, forcing a play-off the following day, which Macfarlane won by a shot.

At the following year's U.S. Open, at Scioto in Ohio, Jones's ball again moved on the green, and he called another penalty shot on himself. Praise was again heaped upon him for his honesty, but he felt this was misplaced. "There is only one way to play the game," he said. "You might as well praise a man for not robbing a bank."

During these, his later years, Jones was universally admired for his approach to the game, but his early days were eventful for other reasons. He was a precocious and hot-headed youth and often threw clubs after a bad shot.

During the third round of his first British Open in 1921 at St. Andrews, he became so frustrated with the eccentricities of the Old Course, in particular the fearsome Hill Bunker on the par-three eleventh hole, that he tore up his scorecard. Forty years later, he wrote: "It was the most inglorious failure of my golfing life."

In 1947, Jones experienced pain in his shoulder, the first signs of syringomyelia, for which there was no cure. Three years later, Jones bumped into an old friend, Al Laney, by which time Jones's right side was completely paralyzed. Laney asked Jones about his health, and Jones replied, "I can tell you there is no help. I know I can only get worse. But you are not to keep thinking of it. You know, in golf we play the ball as it lies. Now, we will not speak of this again, ever."

In 1954, the United States Golf Association (USGA) created

the Bobby Jones Award for distinguished sportsmanship in golf. The first recipient, in 1955, was Francis Ouimet. Other winners include Patti Berg (1963), Roberto de Vicenzo (1970), Arnold Palmer (1971), Jack Nicklaus (1975), Bob Hope and Bing Crosby (1978), Chi Chi Rodriguez (1989), Tom Watson (1987), and Nancy Lopez (1998).

In 1958, Jones was named a Freeman of the City of St. Andrews, becoming only the second American to receive the honor after Benjamin Franklin in 1759. Jones gave his acceptance speech in front of 1,700 people in Younger Hall at the University of St. Andrews. During it, he conceded that his first visit to the Old Course had not been his finest hour, but he hoped he had redeemed himself since.

Any doubts about this were dispelled as Jones left the hall. Golf writer Herbert Warren Wind, who attended the ceremony, wrote in his column in the *New Yorker*:

> At the end of his talk he was helped from the stage to his electric golf car, and as he directed it down the center aisle toward the door the whole hall suddenly burst into the old Scottish song "Will

ye no' come back again?" and it came pouring out with all the wild, overwhelming emotion of a pibroch wailed in some lonesome glen.

Self-belief

............•...............

*Watson scares me. If he's lying six in the middle of the fairway,
there's some kind of way he might make a five.*

LEE TREVINO, *SAN FRANCISCO CHRONICLE*, 1979

*Never give up. If we give up in this game, we'll give
up on life. If you give up that first time, it's easier to
give up the second, third, and fourth times.*

TOM WATSON, *GOLF DIGEST*, 1979

The 1982 U.S. Open at Pebble Beach, California, had been a long and difficult affair. With the course set up to be hard, and the ever-present wind blowing off the Pacific Ocean, birdies had not come easily. And as Tom Watson teed off on the second-to-last hole—tied for the lead with Jack Nicklaus at four under par—things appeared to get a lot more difficult. He pulled his 2-iron long and left, and his ball buried itself deep in the kikuyu grass next to the green. Nicklaus, watching the action on a TV monitor in the clubhouse, breathed easier. Anything worse than two pars from Watson would mean victory for Jack.

Watson arrived at the green and studied his lie, which was not as bad as he had expected it to be. Still, he grimaced. Too cute, and he could leave his ball in the grass. Equally, he could get a flier and find himself more than five yards past the hole. His playing partner, Bill Rogers, stood by and watched. The only sound came from the seagulls wheeling and squawking above Stillwater Bay.

Watson's caddie, Bruce Edwards, told him to get it close. Watson's response was emphatic: "Close? I'm going to make it!" And he did, hacking the ball out of the rough with a sand iron, from where it scurried across the green, hit the flagstick, and disappeared. Watson did a victory jig around the green and looked heavenward. He then birdied the final hole—hitting a three-wood, then a seven-iron and nine-iron to the green, and then holing the putt—to win by two shots.

Watson said of his shot on seventeen: "Playing the shot with an open club face, I hit it just onto the green and watched it break to the right, hit the flagstick dead center and drop in the hole. It meant more to me than any other single shot of my whole life."

Tom Watson's record of eight majors—five British Opens, one U.S. Open, and two Masters—was achieved with a good technique, even swing tempo, strength of character, bold putting, and self-belief. Notably, he was voted the PGA's Player of the Year six times—four times in succession from 1977 to 1980.

He knew how to score, even when he wasn't at his best. Andy Bean wrote in *Golf Digest* in 1984: "When you drive into the left rough, hack your second out into a greenside bunker, come out within six feet of the hole, and sink the slippery putt—when you do that, you've made a Watson par."

Triumph

..............●..............

Palmer usually walks to the first tee quite unlike any other pro on the circuit. He doesn't walk onto it so much as climb into it, almost as though it were a prize ring; and then he looks around at the gallery as though he is trying to count the house.

CHARLES PRICE, *THE WORLD OF GOLF*

His epitaph might well be: "Here lies Arnold Palmer. He always went for the green."

HENRY LONGHURST, *ARNOLD PALMER—A VERY CONSIDERABLE MAN*

Arnold Palmer frowned as he munched on a sandwich before the final round of the 1960 U.S. Open on a hot and sunny Sunday afternoon at Cherry Hills, Colorado. Palmer was lying in fifteenth place, seven shots behind leader Mike Souchak and five behind Ben Hogan. However, he was bothered not by the shots he had to make up to overtake Souchak, but that he had been asked by a journalist whether Souchak could hold on to win.

Palmer responded: "I might shoot 65 out there this afternoon. What'll that do?"

"Nothing," was the retort, "you're too far back."

"No I'm not," Palmer said. "A 65 would give me a total of 280, and doesn't 280 always win the U.S. Open?"

"Yeah, when Hogan shoots it," said Dan Jenkins of the *Fort Worth Press*.

"Watch me," said Palmer. "I'll tell you what I'm going to do. I'm going to drive the first green."

In fact, Palmer had tried to drive the 339-yard first green each day—attempting to take advantage of the thin Colorado air—but had failed every time. On the fourth day, however, he succeeded, crashing a drive onto the green and two-putting for a birdie. He had five more birdies on the next six holes, went out in 30—labeled by some as the greatest nine holes of golf ever played—shot 65, and won by two shots over Jack Nicklaus. Palmer celebrated his final putt by tossing his visor high in the air. His final round remains the greatest comeback in U.S. Open history.

That year, Palmer won eight tournaments, including The Masters after birdying the final two holes to edge out Ken Venturi by a shot. It was the start of an amazing 10 years—at the end of the 1960s, Palmer was named Athlete of the Decade by the Associated Press.

No person has done more for the world's professional golfers than Palmer, who was born in Latrobe, Pennsylvania, in 1929. Aged twenty-four, he won the 1954 U.S. Amateur in Detroit. He immediately stopped selling paint and turned professional, transforming what many saw as a dull post–World War II pastime involving men in strange clothes into a sexy, go-at-the-hole-and-to-hell-with-the-consequences battle. "In a sport that was high society, Palmer made it *High Noon*," said broadcaster Vin Scully.

If Palmer saw a flag tucked behind a bunker next to a lake, he hitched up his trousers, paced about, puffed on a cigarette, then threw it aside and went for it. It mattered not whether he was three shots behind or leading by the same margin.

During a glittering career, Palmer won seven majors, gathered hordes of fans—affectionately called Arnie's Army—became golf's first millionaire, and later launched a stellar business career. Today, he is still feted and charmed, no more so than by the professionals who have benefited from his charisma and now regularly play for weekly purses of up to $6 million.

In 1970, Ken Still wrote in *Golf Magazine*, "He's the reason we're playing for all this money today. Arnie made it all possible. I'll tell you what I think of the man. If he should walk in the door right now and say, 'Shine my shoes,' I'd take off my shirt, get down on my hands and knees, and shine his shoes."

With his make-or-break approach, there were always going to be disasters. Palmer came second in 10 majors, including a record four times in the U.S. Open. But no runner-up finish was worse than the 1966 U.S. Open at the Olympic Club in San Francisco, where Palmer held a seven-shot lead entering the back nine. Pursuing Ben Hogan's record Open score of 276, Palmer leaked shots, eventually tying with Billy

Casper. Palmer lost the play-off by four shots the following day, despite leading by two shots with eight holes to play.

He also took 10 strokes at the seventeenth hole at St. Andrews in the 1960 British Open, and a 12 on the final hole of the 1961 Los Angeles Open. "That will give the duffers a bit of heart," he said, typically.

But perhaps the story that embodies Palmer best involves a tournament at Fort Worth's Colonial Country Club in 1962. As he was taking his stance, Palmer was disturbed by a little boy who was talking to his mother, and he backed away from his ball. The mother put her hand over the boy's mouth. Palmer saw this and said, "Hey, don't choke him. This isn't that important."

Pushing Boundaries

...............•..............

I can beat any two players in this tournament by myself. If I need any help, I'll let you know.

BABE ZAHARIAS, TO HER PARTNER PEGGY KIRK BELL IN A FOUR-BALL
EVENT

It's not enough just to swing at the ball. You've got to loosen your girdle and really let the ball have it.

BABE ZAHARIAS

It was only a matter of time before precocious young Texan girl Mildred Didrikson discovered golf. Then again, perhaps golf discovered her.

Born in 1911, the sixth of seven children to Norwegian immigrants Ole and Hannah in the coastal Texan town of Port Arthur, young Mildred showed extraordinary talent for any sport she turned her hand to, including track and field, basketball, baseball, softball, diving, and rollerskating. She was given the nickname Babe—after Babe Ruth—when she hit five home runs in a junior baseball game. At sixteen, she broke the world javelin record with a throw of 133 feet, 3¼ inches.

When asked if there was anything she didn't play, she replied, "Yes, dolls."

Never one to specialize in one sport when she felt she could dominate all of them, Babe Didrikson qualified for five events at the 1932 Los Angeles Olympic Games but was allowed to enter only three. She made the most of her chances, winning gold medals in the javelin, where she set world and Olympic records with a throw of 143 feet, 4 inches, and the 80-meter hurdles, which she ran in 11.7 seconds, an Olympic record. She won a silver medal in the high jump with a leap of 5 feet, 5 inches.

Didrikson began to play golf in the mid-1930s, a relatively late entry to the game, but her athletic prowess quickly proved a great weapon. Her broad shoulders allowed her to hit the ball prodigious distances, and she built on this by developing a sharp short game. One golf writer said she was "a crushing and heartbreaking opponent."

Babe Didrikson met her husband, professional wrestler George Zaharias, on a golf course in 1938. They married after a quick romance and became a formidable team. Babe liked to do things her way, though it didn't always work out. When she was playing an event in Florida, her ball rolled behind a large stone lion. She called her husband over, told him that the lion was a moveable obstruction, and asked him to shift it. He huffed and puffed but couldn't budge it. Babe had to play around it.

Nor was Babe a stickler for the rules. On one occasion, her playing partner asked if she could get a free drop for a ball lying in some water. "Honey," Babe replied, "I don't care if you send it out and get it dry-cleaned."

Babe Zaharias achieved extraordinary things in women's golf, both as an amateur and a professional, winning a total of 82 tournaments. In the mid-1940s, she won seventeen straight women's amateur titles, a feat never equaled. This streak included the 1946 U.S. Women's Amateur and the 1947 British Women's Amateur—she was the first American woman to win both events. She won three U.S. Women's Opens—in 1948, 1950, and 1954.

Always one for pushing boundaries, Zaharias entered several men's golf competitions and was not shamed. In 1945, she played in three PGA tournaments, making the halfway cut at the Los Angeles Open before finishing thirty-third at the Phoenix Open and tying for forty-second at the Tucson Open.

In 1953, she entered the hospital with bowel cancer and underwent surgery. Despite her discomfort, and the fact that she had lost both weight and strength, she was determined to continue playing. She subsequently entered the 1954 Women's Open at the Salem Country Club in Massachusetts and shot a four-round total of 291 (72, 71, 73, and 75) to win by twelve shots. The last two rounds were played on the same day, and she needed a nap between them, but she announced that she had a good 20 years of golf left in her.

However, her health deteriorated rapidly, and she became bedridden. While spending the Christmas of 1955 in Forth Worth, she asked to see a golf course for the last time.

Her husband and Bertha Bowen, an old friend, drove her to the second green of the Colonial Country Club. Dressed in pajamas, she tottered to the green, knelt down, and laid her hands flat on the grass. She then returned to the car, and the group drove off.

In March 1956, doctors at John Sealy Hospital in Galveston severed her spinal cord to ease her pain. She survived another six months, dying on the morning of September 27, aged forty-five.

Byron Nelson said, "She was the toughest competitor and the most gracious lady I ever met on a golf course."

Size Isn't Everything

Faith has been the primary guideline for my life. But when I'm in a tournament, I don't pray to win. Probably most of the players are doing that. After all, there can only be one winner, and there's no special reason God should pick me to win. Rather, I pray for courage, strength, and guidance.

GARY PLAYER

He was very mystical, a health fanatic who was big on the power of positive thinking. . . . Were he to land in hell, his critics said, he would probably immediately start talking about what a wonderful place it is.

DAN GLEASON, *THE GREAT, THE GRAND AND*

THE ALSO-RAN

After South African Gary Player had beaten Tony Lema on the first play-off hole in the 36-hole semifinal of the 1965 World Match Play Championship at Wentworth, Surrey, having been 7 down with seventeen holes to play and 5 down with nine to play, he said the win "contains my whole life story."

Player had to scrap for everything in his career. Neither blessed with a beautiful golf swing nor a classic grip, he learned to survive through hard work, practice, self-reliance, courage, and faith. His diminutive size—5'7" and 145 pounds—meant he couldn't hit the ball a long way, but he treated this as merely another challenge to be overcome. He lifted weights, ran regularly, and ate a strict diet. He practiced harder than anyone, and he listened to advice.

It was no coincidence that Player's greatest strength was his bunker play—golf's ultimate scrambling shot. Player's sand wedge got him out of countless jams and became a stake in the heart of a multitude of opponents.

Player scrambled from the moment he flew to the UK in the mid-1950s as a raw 19-year-old. He was criticized not only for his swing and his grip, but for his clothes and hairstyle. Some local pros told him to pack up and go home. He missed more cuts than he made and many years later wrote in his book *Grand Slam Golf*, "I was very bitter and shaken by this first experience of British golf. But it did a great service to my drive and determination."

Player did what he has always done during adversity—he worked harder.

In 1957, despite the fact that he had very little money, he decided to try the US tour, often hitching between tournaments. The following year, he came in second to Tommy Bolt in the U.S. Open at Southern Hills and won $5000, kick-starting his career.

In 1959, Player won the British Open at Muirfield, despite trailing the leader by eight shots after two rounds. He shot 70 and 68 in the final thirty-six holes, despite a double-bogey 6 on the last hole. His opponents fell away, and, when he finally realized he had won the tournament, he sat on the podium for half an hour before the presentation to soak up the moment.

The next two decades saw Player win eight more majors: two more British Opens, a U.S. Open, three Masters, and two PGAs. He was dominant enough to be linked with Jack Nicklaus and Arnold Palmer, and they were collectively known as "The Big Three."

Above all, Player was a trailblazer. Over five decades of

competitive golf, he travelled more than 15 million miles and won 165 tournaments, including seven Australian Opens, five World Match Play titles, and the small matter of thirteen South African Opens. Somewhere along the way, he and his wife, Vivienne, managed to have six children.

Player's record in America, as a non-American, was phenomenal. Only one non-American won The Masters between its conception in 1934 and 1980, and that was Player. In fact, he won it in 1961, 1974, and 1978, setting the scene for other non-American winners, including Seve Ballesteros, Jose Maria Olazabal, Nick Faldo, Ian Woosnam, and Sandy Lyle.

Player describes himself in *Grand Slam Golf* as "small, dark, deliberate, painstaking . . . a man without talent who has done it all by sheer hard work and nothing else." Many others have since emulated his work ethic. Player's aphorism for hard work—"The more I practice, the luckier I get"—has become the mantra of thousands of wannabe professionals worldwide.

He is one of only five golfers to have won all four majors, sitting alongside Gene Sarazen, Ben Hogan, Jack Nicklaus, and Tiger Woods. That alone puts him in a small—and very rare—orbit.

After his remarkable semifinal comeback against Tony Lema at the 1965 World Match Play Championship, Player came up against Australian Peter Thomson in the final. Thomson was fresh from his fifth British Open win at Royal Birkdale and was playing fine golf.

Player won 3 and 2.

"Player was a tough nut to crack," Thomson says. "You didn't get off lightly with him. He played with a great intensity which was very confronting. There weren't many smiles and pats on the back. He mis-hit some shots but didn't miss too many putts. His short game was particularly brilliant."

Perspective

..............●..............

Not really. After all, I put it there.

WALTER HAGEN, TO A SPECTATOR WHO MENTIONED
THE BAD LUCK OF HIS LIE

Like life, golf can be humbling. However, little good comes from
brooding about mistakes we've made.
The next shot, in golf or in life, is the big one.

GRANTLAND RICE, *THE TUMULT AND THE SHOUTING*

Roberto de Vicenzo's forty-fifth birthday on April 14, 1968, happened to coincide with the final round of The Masters, and he was in the hunt. The Argentine started, miraculously, with an eagle 2, and the crowd celebrated by singing him happy birthday.

The former *lagunero* (pond boy)—his first job in Buenos Aires as a boy was to retrieve golf balls from lakes and ditches—played the first nine in thirty-one shots, five under par, before he picked up two more shots on the twelfth and fifteenth. He hit his second shot on the seventeenth to six-and-a-half and made the putt for another birdie. He bogeyed the final hole, but his 65 was good enough to tie with Bob Goalby, a handsome one-time football player from Illinois, for first place. A play-off would take place the next day.

A few minutes after walking off the final green, de Vicenzo signed his scorecard without noticing that his playing partner, Tommy Aaron, had entered a 4 instead of a 3 for the seventeenth hole. Above de Vicenzo's signature on the scorecard were printed the words: "I have checked my score hole by hole."

The rules committee—Ike Grainger, John Winters, and Hord Hardin—consulted with the bedridden Bobby Jones, who was in the final stages of his battle with syringomyelia. The ruling was unambiguous: any player who signs for a score on a hole that is higher than the score he actually shot must take the higher score. Officials determined that de Vicenzo had shot a 66, despite the fact that he clearly played 65 strokes. Goalby was declared the winner.

"I'm very happy I won the tournament," Goalby said, "and I'd be a liar if I told you I wasn't. But I'm really sorry I won it the way I did. I'd much rather have done it in a play-off. Roberto has been one of my good friends for twelve years."

Grainger and de Vicenzo dined together that evening, and the Argentine apologized for the trouble he had caused. "What a stupid I am," he later told the media in his trademark faltering English. "I just signed a wrong card. But I congratulate Bob Goalby. He gave me so much pressure that I lose my brain. I think maybe I make a few friends. That means more than money. What is money, anyway?"

In 1970, de Vicenzo received the Bobby Jones Award for distinguished sportsmanship in golf.

Consistency

..............●..............

Tam arte quam marte: As much by skill as by strength.

CLUB MOTTO, ROYAL TROON GOLF CLUB, SCOTLAND

Don't let the bad shots get to you. Don't let yourself become angry. The
true scramblers are thick-skinned. And they always beat the whiners.

PAUL RUNYAN, *GOLF DIGEST*, 1977

Australian Peter Thomson was the only golfer to win three
consecutive British Opens in the twentieth century—in 1954,
1955, and 1956. He also won the tournament in 1958 and 1965,

his five victories matching the records of James Braid and J.H. Taylor; later, Tom Watson would emulate the feat. Only one man did better: Harry Vardon, who won the British Open six times.

Just as extraordinary as Thomson's five wins in this fiercely contested tournament was his overall consistency in the event throughout the 1950s and 1960s. From 1951, when he was twenty years old, to 1971, Thomson's placings at the British Open were: tied for sixth, second, tied for second, first, first, first, second, first, tied for twenty-third, tied for ninth, tied for seventh, tied for sixth, fifth, tied for twenty-fourth, first, tied for eighth, tied for eighth, tied for twenty-fourth, tied for third, tied for ninth, and tied for ninth.

During that period, Thomson finished in the Open's top ten eighteen times. In one seven-year spell—1952 to 1958—he finished either first or second.

The story of Thomson's first British Open win in 1954 not only conjures a different time, but shows a man who marched to a very different drummer.

"I had been playing in the United States for the previous six months with MacGregor irons, which I was under contract to play with," says Thomson. "They had very small heads, and the day before the Open started, I decided I couldn't win with them." Thomson approached Glasgow-based club maker John Letters, who was in Birkdale showing off his wares, and asked if he had a spare set of clubs. "He got a set out of his car, I hit a few balls with them and then used them the next day."

He won the title by a shot from Sid Scott, Dai Rees, and Bobby Locke. After being presented with the famous claret jug and a check for £750—"a small fortune back then," says Thomson— he returned the clubs to Letters. Did he think of keeping them? "Heavens no, I had only borrowed them," he says.

Thomson, who ultimately won 86 tournaments world- wide, including the national opens of ten countries, says his consistency in the British Open was the result of preparation and affinity:

> Each year I prepared for the British Open for months. It loomed large in my dreams and my forward planning. I seemed to have a special aptitude for the British seaside links. They were hard and fast, like the course I grew up on in Australia, and the bounce of the ball was important.

A lot of Americans who came over for the event didn't know what it was all about. I analysed each course, sorted out where the trouble was, and worked out how to keep away from it. Then it was a matter of repeating a good swing. Common sense and sensible living—that's the key. The super player has one vital quality, calmness.

Patience

............•.............

*The Senior Tour is like a class reunion. It's the same
as it was thirty years ago. We tell the same dirty
jokes—only they're funnier now.*

BOB TOSKI, *GOLF DIGEST*, 1983

*I really haven't given it much thought. After all, I won't become
eligible for another 42 months, five days,
and eight-and-a-half hours.*

BUTCH BAIRD, WHEN ASKED IF HE WOULD JOIN THE U.S. SENIOR PGA
TOUR, *GOLF DIGEST*, 1983

Walt Zembriski taught himself to play golf in the 1940s and 1950s while working as a caddie at Out of Bounds Golf Club in Mahwah, New Jersey. He earned his US tour player's card in 1967 and had a brief and largely uninspiring career, failing to win any tournaments.

Zembriski left the tour in his midthirties and took a job as an ironworker on high-rise buildings in New Jersey. He still loved the game and played part-time during his forties on the Florida minitour. He won a few events, even qualifying for the 1978 and 1982 U.S. Opens but mostly pocketed around $500 or $600 a week. By the early 1980s, he was living out of his 1964 Buick and was down to one pair of red pants with a hole in them.

Then, in 1985, a magical thing happened—Zembriski turned fifty, and he became eligible for the U.S. Senior PGA Tour.

Now called the Champions Tour, the Senior PGA Tour was the brainchild of Sam Snead, Julius Boros, Gardner Dickinson, Bob Goalby, Don January, and Dan Sikes. They met in January 1980 and planned two tournaments a year for golfers over fifty, each with a purse of $170,000. The public, they reasoned, would be interested in watching great golfers from years past.

The winners of the first two tournaments were January, then aged fifty, and 58-year-old Charlie Sifford, each picking up $27,000. By 1984, there were twenty-four tournaments each year offering more than $7 million in prize money. "If you'd told me back in 1980 that we'd have this many events and be playing for this much money, I'd have said you were crazy," said January.

Zembriski had not played golf as much as the other members of the Senior Tour, most of whom had played the regular PGA Tour for around twenty years, but the time spent dabbling on the Florida minitour had kept his game sharp, and several years of lugging iron on construction sites had strengthened his muscles and helped him maintain his fitness.

Not long after turning fifty, Zembriski played in the 1985 U.S. Senior Open in Lake Tahoe and finished fourth, winning $9,000. He went on to win a total of $47,000 that year in prize money, and more than $100,000 in 1986 and again in 1987. In 1988, aged fifty-three, he won both the Newport Cup and the Vantage Championship, and in 1989 he won the GTE West Classic. As a result of his patience and perseverance, he pocketed $2.3 million.

"Walt is an example of what can happen if you're a pretty

good player," Arnold Palmer told *Sports Illustrated*. "He played the minitour and had some success, took that experience and applied it to the Senior Tour. He's a scrapper, a player of great endurance. I think it's great that a man can come right off the street—if he can play—and enjoy a lifestyle he's never had."

Zembriski says his time in the building trade had other advantages: "Once you've walked a 6-inch beam fifty floors off the ground, a 3-foot putt doesn't scare you."

Today, the Champions Tour includes twenty-six events held in the United States, Britain, the Dominican Republic, Canada, and South Korea. The total prize money is more than $51 million, with an average purse of $1.98 million.

Attention to Detail

..............●..............

The terrible thing about a missed shot in golf is that the thing is done, irrevocably, irretrievable. Perhaps that is why golf is so great a game; it is so much like the game of life. We don't have the shots over in either.

O.B. KEELER, ATLANTA SPORTSWRITER

The world's number one tennis player spends 90 percent of his time winning, while the world's number one golfer spends 90 percent of his time losing. Golfers are great losers.

DAVID FEHERTY, JOURNEYMAN PROFESSIONAL

On the last day of the 2001 British Open at Royal Lytham & St. Annes, Welshman Ian Woosnam hit his tee shot at the par-three opening hole to within a few inches and tapped in for a birdie to tie for the lead. It was the perfect start to the final round of his nation's championship. However, by the time he teed off on the next hole, Woosnam had dropped two shots.

"You're going to go ballistic," Woosnam's caddie, Miles Byrne, told his player on the second tee, before revealing that there were fifteen clubs in Woosnam's bag—one more than the rules of golf allow. Woosnam incurred an immediate two-stroke penalty and did indeed go ballistic, which didn't help his golf. He recorded bogeys on two of the next three holes and eventually tied for third behind the winner, American David Duval.

Woosnam won £141,666 in prize money. Had he finished second, he would have collected £360,000. Who knows what he might have achieved without the bad news he received on the second tee.

"It's the biggest mistake he will make in his life. He won't do it again," Woosnam said of Byrne after the tournament.

Two weeks later, Woosnam sacked Byrne with immediate effect after his caddie appeared late for the early-morning final round of the Scandinavian Masters.

Quick Thinking

............●.............

People say it was amazing that Jimmy Demaret could win three
Masters almost without practicing. I think it's amazing he would
win them almost without sleeping.

SAM SNEAD, *GOLF DIGEST*, 1983

That's what caused both of my divorces, spending
too much time with Jimmy.

LEE TREVINO, *LEGENDS OF GOLF,* NBC-TV, 1984

Shortly after World War II, Seminole Golf Club in Florida
began holding an annual two-day pro-am, which most of the

well-known golfers attended. The tournament was run by the club's professional, 1948 Masters winner Claude Harmon.

One day during the tournament, tour playboy Jimmy Demaret, whose colorful wardrobe was matched only by the company he kept, arrived at the Seminole front gate with his pal Vic Ghezzi and two female companions. The guards wouldn't let them proceed because the tournament was a men-only event. Demaret, never one to back away from a challenge, rang Harmon.

"Hey Claude, we've got a couple of friends with us and the guards won't let us in," Demaret complained. "What's going on?"

"These friends of yours, are they pros?" Harmon asked.

After a short pause, Demaret replied, "Er, yes, Claude, they're pros."

Sportsmanship

..............●..............

Golf is the Esperanto of sport. All over the world golfers talk the same language . . . endure the same frustrations, discover the same infallible secrets of putting, share the same illusory joys.

HENRY LONGHURST, *ROUND IN SIXTY-EIGHT*, 1953

I saw two spike marks on my line. It looked a left, a left putt. I talked to my caddie. He said, "Hit it left center and firm to avoid the spike marks." That's what I tried to do. It did not go in.

GERMAN BERNHARD LANGER ON THE FOUR-FOOT PUTT HE MISSED TO
BEAT HALE IRWIN AND RETURN THE RYDER CUP TO EUROPE, 1991

Yorkshire seed merchant Samuel Ryder took up golf late in life, and only for health reasons, so it is in some ways surprising that his name has become synonymous with one of the greatest of the world's golfing rivalries.

In the early 1900s, Ryder had become very wealthy selling packets of seeds, but his health was suffering due to overwork, and his doctor suggested he get more exercise and fresh air. He took up golf and hired English professional Abe Mitchell as his private coach, on a salary of £1,000 a year.

Ryder threw himself into his new passion, practicing hard, and within a year had obtained a six handicap. In 1923, he sponsored the Heath and Heather Tournament, open only to professionals.

Three years later, when Ryder was well into his seventies, he witnessed Mitchell and other British golfers, including George Duncan, Archie Compston, and Ted Ray, beat a team of Americans—including Walter Hagen, Tommy Armour, Jim Barnes, and Al Watrous—at Wentworth outside London.

Ryder loved the concept of a regular international match between the two countries and commissioned a gold cup, with a likeness of Mitchell on the top, to be competed for every two years between a team of American professionals and a team from Britain and Ireland.

The first official Ryder Cup—including foursomes and singles matches only—was played in 1927 at the Worcester Country Club in Massachusetts. Walter Hagen captained the American team and Ted Ray the British/Irish team. The Americans triumphed, 9.5 to 2.5.

The early years of the Ryder Cup were lopsided affairs. Of the first seventeen matches—between 1927 and 1967—the American team won fourteen of them. The British wins came in 1929 and 1933, and then nearly a quarter of a century later in 1957.

In 1967, in Houston, Texas, the Americans trounced the visitors, 23.5 points to 8.5, in the expanded format, made up of foursomes, fourball, and singles. The result was not unexpected: the American team was captained by Ben Hogan and included Billy Casper, Arnold Palmer, Gay Brewer, Al Geiberger, Julius Boros, Gene Littler, and Doug Sanders.

Two years later, at Royal Birkdale in northern England, there seemed to be a different feeling about the contest, despite the fact that the Americans had won the past five Ryder Cups. Twenty-year-old Scot Bernard Gallacher was talking tough.

"I'm not awed by the Americans," he said. "I think maybe they should be awed by me."

"The British are so keyed up they'll be hitting the ball nine million miles," said American player Frank Beard, the leading money winner on the US tour at the time. "And we don't dare go back home if we lose." Although the American team had lost some of its stars, the replacements included Lee Trevino, Tommy Aaron, Ray Floyd, and Jack Nicklaus.

Remarkably, after two-and-a-half days, the British/Irish team led, 13 points to 11, with only an afternoon of singles—with 8 points up for grabs—remaining. A huge upset was in the offing. Feelings were running high after the British/Irish team captain Eric Brown instructed his players not to look for American balls in the rough.

The Americans came out fighting on the final afternoon. Dave Hill beat Brian Barnes, 4 and 2; Miller Barber trounced Maurice Bembridge, 7 and 6; Gene Littler got the better of Christy O'Connor, 2 and 1; and Dan Sikes overcame Neil Coles, 4 and 3. However, Trevino lost to Bernard Gallacher, 4 and 3, and Dale Douglass lost to Britain's Peter Butler.

When Brian Huggett coaxed in a 4-foot putt on the last green to halve his match with Billy Casper, the teams were locked at 15.5 points apiece. It all came down to the final match between Englishman Tony Jacklin, the newly crowned British Open champion, and the best golfer of the era, Jack Nicklaus, who was playing in his first Ryder Cup. Notably, in the morning, Jacklin had beaten Nicklaus, 4 and 3, and had dropped only half a point in four matches.

The pair were all square as they drove off the final tee. Nicklaus played to the green first, and his ball finished 30 feet from the hole, while Jacklin hit to the back of the green. Jacklin putted to two feet, while Nicklaus's birdie putt, for the match, slid three-and-a-half feet past. The crowd of 20,000 held its collective breath as Nicklaus stood over his return putt. "I was terrified," he later conceded. "I wasn't just putting for me, I was putting for my country."

He made the putt, then reached down and picked up Jacklin's ball marker and handed it to him, saying, "I am sure you would have holed, but I wasn't prepared to see you miss." The conceded putt meant their game was halved. The two teams scored 16 points each—the first halved tie in the Ryder Cup's 42-year history—and the cup returned to America.

Although American Captain Sam Snead was none too pleased with Nicklaus's largesse, the American's sportsmanship is remembered, and applauded, to this day. "It was a wonderful sporting gesture, something certainly I'll never forget," Jacklin said.

Thirty years later, Nicklaus and Jacklin designed a course together in Sarasota, Florida. Its name—The Concession.

Courage

..............●..............

So many things about Hogan were special. He was the greatest shot maker I ever saw. He probably worked harder than anyone to reach the top, and it took him a long time. Then, when he got there, his body was all but destroyed by the car accident. All he did was start over again at nearly forty and got even better. Nobody was like Hogan.

JACK NICKLAUS, FROM *BEN HOGAN: THE MAN*
BEHIND THE MYSTIQUE

Ben Hogan invented practice.

DAN JENKINS

On a foggy Texas morning in February 1949, on Highway 80 near Van Horn, not far from the Mexican border, a Greyhound bus on the Dallas–El Paso run pulled out onto the wrong side of the road to overtake a large truck. Traveling the other way were Ben Hogan and his wife, Valerie. Hogan saw the bus coming, but a guardrail prevented him from veering away. The bus collided with the front left-hand side of Hogan's Cadillac.

Valerie emerged relatively unscathed from the crash, but Hogan was a mess. He had broken his collarbone and fractured his pelvis, a rib, and his left ankle. Later, a blood clot formed in his right lung, and a vascular surgeon was brought in to tie off a major vein in his leg to prevent more clots. His doctors said he might never walk again, let alone play golf competitively. It seemed that the 36-year-old's career, which included two PGAs and the previous year's U.S. Open, was over.

Hogan eventually left the hospital on April 1, fifty-nine days after the accident. He began his serious recuperation by walking laps around the living room of his Fort Worth home. He putted most days, then eventually began to hit longer shots. Toward the end of 1949, he played his first full round of golf, then spent the rest of the day in bed recovering.

Hogan returned to competitive golf in January 1950 at

the Los Angeles Open. Nine thousand people turned up on the opening day—a record—to see Hogan. The other players, one writer said, "roamed the acres unmolested." Hogan eventually lost to Sam Snead in a play-off. Said golf writer Grantland Rice, "His legs simply were not strong enough to carry around his heart."

Five months later, Hogan travelled to Merion Golf Club in Philadelphia to compete in the fiftieth U.S. Open. No one was sure whether his battered legs would stand up to the 36-hole double round on the final day. To soothe his aching legs before playing a round, Hogan would soak in a hot bath for an hour before having them rubbed and then swathed in elastic bandaging. Finally, he'd wash down an aspirin with orange juice or ginger ale.

Hogan and Valerie booked into the Barclay Hotel a week before the tournament started, and Hogan got to work practicing. Merion members will tell you that, when playing the short eighth hole on one of his practice rounds, Hogan drove to a plateau over the fairway bunker on the right. He played his second to the green, then told his caddie, "Make sure you replace the divot carefully. I plan to be here every round." He also famously left his seven-iron out of his bag for the tournament, saying, "There are no seven-iron shots at Merion."

Hogan played the first round in 72 strokes, two over par. It wasn't earth-shattering, but it did him no harm. A second-round 69 put him in fifth spot, behind Dutch Harrison, Johnny Bulla, Jim Ferrier, and Julius Boros. Hogan vomited on the way home and conceded to Valerie back at the hotel that he doubted his ability to play thirty-six holes the following day.

After a third-round 72 the next morning, he moved up to tie for second alongside Johnny Palmer and Cary Middlecoff, two strokes behind new leader Lloyd Mangrum. In the afternoon round, he played the front nine in one over par, but this was enough to eke out a three-stroke lead. The pain was getting to him, and he often stopped to grasp his legs when negotiating steep hills. On several occasions, Middlecoff, Hogan's playing partner, removed Hogan's ball from the hole for him. On the twelfth hole, his legs cramped on his drive, and he was forced to grab Middlecoff's arm for support. He later conceded that he had considered pulling out then and there.

Legend has it that, on the thirteenth green, after holing out for par, Hogan turned to his caddie and said that he was finished, instructing the caddie to take the clubs back to the clubhouse. The caddie reportedly responded, "No Mr Hogan, I don't work for quitters. I'll see you on the fourteenth tee, sir."

Hogan made a par on the fourteenth and then three-putted from seven feet on the fifteenth. He parred the sixteenth and bogeyed the seventeenth, and by the time he reached the eighteenth tee, his lead was gone. After a good drive, he was left with a 220-yard shot to the green. Fred Corcoran, who ran the US tour, told Hogan that the best score in was 287, by both George Fazio and Mangrum. A par would tie for the lead.

Hogan selected a one-iron and played the most important shot of his career, to the left front of the green, about 50 feet from the pin. He two-putted for par.

Hogan's shot to the green was immortalized in a photo taken by *Life* magazine's Hy Peskin, which now sits on thousands of desks around the world as a lesson in fortitude and courage. The photo shows the green and fairway surrounded by spectators whose eyes are following the flight of the ball. Hogan's follow-through is balanced and powerful and gives no indication of the pain he was in.

Today, a modest stone plaque sits on the eighteenth fairway at Merion. It reads: "June 11, 1950. U.S. Open, Fourth Round, Ben Hogan, One Iron." Alongside the plaque is the invariable collection of divots made by golfers attempting to emulate Hogan.

The day after his one-iron shot, Hogan won the 18-hole play-off, shooting 69 to Mangrum's 73 and Fazio's 75. "I'm just so relieved to have it done," Hogan said afterward.

However, Hogan now practiced harder than ever, despite his injuries. He hit balls until his hands bled. *Time* magazine likened his swing, and the result, to "stamping out bottle caps." The following year—1951—he won his first Masters and his third U.S. Open, closing with a 67 at Oakland Hills, perhaps the finest round of his career.

In 1953, aged forty, he had his greatest year, winning The Masters again, then his fourth U.S. Open at a brutal Oakmont, and finally the British Open at Carnoustie, Scotland, in his first and only attempt. When he returned to the United States, he received a ticker tape parade on New York's Broadway.

Many sought interviews with the courageous champion, and Hogan, a man of few words, gave them reluctantly. When asked for advice for young players, he often responded: "Watch out for buses."

Daring

...........•...........

Seve's never in trouble. We see him in the trees quite
a lot, but that looks normal to him.

BEN CRENSHAW, *SPORTS ILLUSTRATED*, 1983

I look into their eyes, shake their hand, pat their
back, and wish them luck, but I am thinking,
"I am going to bury you."

SEVE BALLESTEROS, ON HIS OPPONENTS

With one hole to go in the 1993 European Masters at Crans-sur-
Sierre, high in the Swiss Alps, Spaniard Severiano Ballesteros

was only a shot behind the leaders. But on the eighteenth, he blocked his drive right and grimaced in frustration.

Five minutes later, when Ballesteros and his caddie, Billy Foster, found the ball, things did not look good. The ball was only seven feet away from the 10-foot-high wall protecting the club's swimming pool. Branches from a pine tree hung over the wall, presenting what seemed an impenetrable obstacle to the green, about 130 yards away.

Foster informed Ballesteros that his only option was to take his medicine, chip out sideways, and try to make par from the fairway. Seeing a chink of light above the wall, Ballesteros muttered something to Foster that included the word "maybe" and grabbed a club from the bag.

Foster decided that his player had lost his marbles and, realizing that an argument was futile, backed away, shaking his head. As he waited for Ballesteros to size up the shot, Foster glanced down at the bag and was staggered to see that the sand wedge was still in it. Ballesteros had taken a less-lofted wedge.

The caddie closed his eyes and uttered a silent prayer, convinced that the ricocheting ball would either kill Ballesteros outright or at the very least put him in the hospital. Ballesteros swung as hard as he could. The ball flew high, clearing the wall and threading the branches, and landed on the edge of the green . . . from where he chipped in for a birdie.

When Ballesteros started his career in the mid-1970s, Americans dominated world golf. Of the 40 major championships played during that decade, Americans won 33 of them. And they were almost unbeatable at The Masters. Only one non-American, South African Gary Player, won the tournament between 1934, its first year, and 1980.

But then Ballesteros, the 23-year-old farmer's son from Pedreña in Spain, changed everything. In the 1980 event, he opened with a 66, shot 275, and won by four shots from Gibby Gilbert and Australian Jack Newton. Europeans then won 10 of the next 19 Masters.

Quite simply, Ballesteros gave his fellow Europeans and other non-Americans the confidence that they could mix it up with the golfing bullies from over the Atlantic. Non-Americans began winning more majors, and Europe started flexing its muscles in the biannual teams match it fought out with the United States, the Ryder Cup.

Ballesteros was not just the best player in the world for ten years, but also the most flamboyant, irrepressible, and charismatic, known for his go-for-broke drives, swashbuckling

85

irons, and an exquisite short game. He also made jaw-dropping recovery shots, such as the one on the final hole of the 1993 European Masters. When asked afterward for his reasoning that day, Ballesteros replied, "I like to go forwards."

The committee of Crans-sur-Sierre erected a plaque to commemorate the shot and roped off the area to prevent golfers from trying to emulate it.

Ballesteros died in May 2011, aged 54.

Brilliance

...........•...........

I had a stretch there for a few years where I played some golf that
bordered on the Twilight Zone . . . I can remember that I was getting
upset that I had to putt.

JOHNNY MILLER, *GOLF MAGAZINE*, 1982

Serenity is knowing that your worst shot is still
going to be pretty good.

JOHNNY MILLER, *SPORTS ILLUSTRATED*, 1975

When steel magnate Henry Fownes designed Oakmont Country
Club in Pennsylvania in the early 1900s, he had one thing in

mind—making a course that would be the toughest in the world. He did pretty well. The course had 220 bunkers (today it has considerably fewer), and each was raked by a device, also designed by Fownes, that created furrows two inches deep and two inches apart. Jimmy Demaret was moved to say: "You could have combed North Africa with it and Rommel wouldn't have got past Casablanca."

The greens were feared more than the bunkers. Fownes insisted they be rolled with barrels of sand weighing a quarter of a ton, then cut to a sixteenth of an inch. The area within seven feet of the cup was cut to a thirty-second of an inch. They were never watered. People regularly three-putted, and four and five putts were not uncommon.

Golf's best players—Tommy Armour, Ben Hogan, Jack Nicklaus, Johnny Miller, Larry Nelson, Ernie Els—have won U.S. Opens at Oakmont, but the wins have never been easy.

Armour won the 1927 U.S. Open without breaking par—he shot 76 in the play-off, which was good enough to win by three strokes. Bobby Jones, the defending champion and the best player around, was not able to break 76 in any of his rounds.

In 1935, Sam Parks was the only player to break 300 when

he won—he shot 299. With two holes to go, Jimmy Thomson, tied with Parks, drove the par-four dogleg seventeenth, then four-putted. He recalled:

> I could have six-putted. When the ball got to two feet from the hole, I thought I had an eagle. Then it took off again. I had to hole a three-footer for my bogey. On the fifth green I had spotted my ball with a dime so Parks could putt out. When I got back to the ball the dime was gone. It had slid off the green.

Things didn't get easier in later years. When Hogan won the U.S. Open at Oakmont in 1953, he bettered par by only one stroke, and in 1962, Jack Nicklaus tied with Arnold Palmer and won the play-off the next day by shooting par.

All this history makes 26-year-old Johnny Miller's winning round on June 17, 1973 all the more remarkable. Miller came to the U.S. Open with only two tour victories in four years. Drawn to play the first two rounds with Arnold Palmer, he shot 71 and 69. Things unravelled in the third round when he played the first eight holes without his yardage book (his wife Linda had to pick it up at the hotel and deliver it to him midround) and shot 76.

Miller started the final day six shots behind the four leading players—Jon Schlee, Arnold Palmer, Julius Boros, and Jerry Heard—with another seven players in front of him, including Nicklaus, Gary Player, Lee Trevino, Tom Weiskopf, and Bob Charles. He birdied the first four holes, making putts of five feet, six inches, 16 feet, and two inches. Five more birdies (on the ninth, eleventh, twelfth, thirteenth, and fifteenth), eight pars, and one solitary bogey followed, giving Miller the victory by a single shot from Schlee.

His final round 63 was the lowest total ever to win a U.S. Open and tied for the lowest round ever shot in a major championship. It was also, needless to say, a course record for Oakmont; the members were not quite sure how it had been accomplished. Miller hit all eighteen greens in regulation and had 29 putts, missing a 13-foot birdie putt on the seventeenth and a 10-foot birdie putt on the eighteenth. The other players in the field that day shot an average of 76; only four other players broke par.

It's considered to be the best competitive round of golf ever played. "I don't know how you can hit it any better under

Open pressure, the last day against a tough field, all those Hall of Famers in front of me," Miller recalled before the U.S. Open returned to Oakmont in 2007. "Every hole, right at the pin, dead underneath the hole, 18 times, average about nine feet from the hole. Sounds like I'm bragging, but the bottom line, it was a crazy round."

Anything's Possible

............•.............

*I don't think I had enough sense to know what
pressure was.*

GENE SARAZEN, *THE NEW YORKER*, 1982

*Luck may be the residue of careful planning, as the wise men say, or
it can be just plain luck.*

GENE SARAZEN, *THIRTY YEARS OF CHAMPIONSHIP GOLF*

At 5:30 p.m. on the afternoon of April 7, 1935, during the final
round of the second Masters (then called the Augusta National
Invitational), Gene Sarazen stood next to his caddie on the
right-hand side of the par-five fifteenth fairway at Augusta and

sized up his second shot. He was about 220 yards out, and the pond in front of the green meant that the shot would have to be all carry.

A minute or so earlier, a roar had come from the eighteenth green. The news came fast: Craig Wood had birdied the final hole and recorded a total of 282. "As we neared the crest of the hill, I squinted at the clubhouse in the distance, where the photographers were snapping pictures of the happy winner and the newspapermen were hurrying to bat out their stories on Craig's victory," Sarazen recalled in his autobiography, *Thirty Years of Championship Golf.*

Sarazen was three strokes behind Wood. He asked his caddie, whose nickname was Stovepipe, what would be needed to win. Stovepipe groaned. "You need four threes, Mr. Gene. Three, three, three, three." He didn't sound confident.

As Sarazen mulled over his club selection, his traditional Cheshire Cat smile became a thin line of concentration. "Mr. Gene, you got to hit the three-wood if you want to clear that water," Stovepipe whispered. Sarazen's playing partner, Walter Hagen, piped up from across the fairway: "Hey, hurry up, Gene. I got a date tonight."

Sarazen pulled out the four-wood, a new model called the

Turfrider, with a hollow-back sole. "I took my stance with my four-wood and rode into the shot with every ounce of strength and timing I could muster. It tore for the flag on a very low trajectory, no more than 30 feet in the air," Sarazen wrote.

The ball cleared the water easily, landed short of the pin, and rolled into the hole for an albatross two (known in the United States as a double eagle). The crowd went mad. Sarazen beamed and waved. Hagen stood there dumbfounded.

The scorer in the clubhouse couldn't make sense of the relayed news. He admonished the kid who had breathlessly passed on the news: "He can't have scored a two on fifteen, surely you mean sixteen."

Sarazen parred the remaining holes to finish level with Wood, then won the 36-hole play-off the following day, shooting 144 to Wood's 149.

He would later call the shot "lucky," but nonetheless, Sarazen's albatross captured the public's imagination and it launched The Masters as a legitimate tournament. The media called it the "shot heard round the world." Never in his wildest dreams could the founder of the tournament, Bobby Jones, who witnessed the shot from a small rise beside the fifteenth green, have envisaged a better way to put his fledgling tournament on the map.

In 1922, aged only twenty, Sarazen had won the U.S. Open at Skokie, outside Chicago. He ended up winning two U.S. Opens (1922 and 1932), one British Open (1932), three PGAs (1922, 1923, and 1933) and the 1935 Masters. He sits alongside Ben Hogan, Jack Nicklaus, Gary Player, and Tiger Woods as the only winners of all four major championships.

But despite his extraordinary career, Sarazen is remembered mainly for his albatross/double eagle, a fact that rankled him until he died in May 1999, aged ninety-seven: "You know, I won the U.S. Open and the British Open and the PGA and I don't know what all, and yet wherever I go, you'd think I'd made only one shot in my life."

That said, Sarazen was always a little surprised that the shot was not recognized by a plaque—or something—on the fifteenth hole. The day after the play-off, he asked Stovepipe whether there was any talk around the club about possible plans to preserve the famous divot mark.

"Mr Gene," Stovepipe drawled, "they went down there this morning, some of the greenkeepers I mean, and they done sprinkled a little rye seed in the divot and covered it up."

Dreaming

............●............

He enjoys that perfect peace, that peace beyond all understanding,
which comes at its maximum to the man who has given up golf.

PG WODEHOUSE

It is the constant and undying hope for improvement that makes golf
so exquisitely worth the playing.

BERNARD DARWIN, BRITISH GOLF WRITER

In the mid-1970s, Maurice Flitcroft, a 46-year-old shipyard crane operator from Barrow-in-Furness on the western coast of England, had a dream—to achieve "fame and fortune by playing in the British Open with Jack Nicklaus and all that lot." That he had never even picked up a golf club did not deter him. He had, he reasoned, always been good at sport, and golf did not look that difficult.

Flitcroft bought a half-set of clubs by mail order, studied a Peter Alliss golf manual that he got from the local library, and pored over instructional articles by 1966 PGA winner Al Geiberger. He practiced with his woods and irons on nearby playing fields and rehearsed bunker shots on a beach. Occasionally, he snuck onto a local course and played a few holes. Satisfied that his game was ready, Flitcroft entered the qualifying rounds at Formby in Liverpool for the 1976 British Open. As he had no handicap, Flitcroft chose the other option on the entry form: professional.

Flitcroft's unsuspecting playing partner, Jim Howard, described his first hole: "After gripping the club like he was intent on murdering someone, Flitcroft hoisted it straight up, came down vertically, and the ball travelled precisely four feet."

His second shot was a shank.

Howard alerted the Royal and Ancient officials who ran the tournament, but despite being both embarrassed and furious, they could do nothing.

Flitcroft's final score of 121, 49 over par, was the worst score recorded in the tournament's 141-year history. One witness described the round as a "blizzard of triple and quadruple bogeys ruined by a solitary par." Howard conceded that the final tally was a little gray, as he had lost count on a couple of holes. The Royal and Ancient officials returned Howard's entry fee.

Flitcroft maintained the score "weren't a fair reflection" of his play and said his swing that day was affected by "lumbago and fibrositis." He also said he had stupidly left his four-wood in his car. "I was an expert with the four-wood, deadly accurate," he said some years later.

Flitcroft's mother took umbrage at the newspapers' reporting of her son's escapade, saying, "Well, he's got to start somewhere, hasn't he?"

The Royal and Ancient Golf Club amended the championship's entry rules to prevent such a thing happening again, but undeterred, Flitcroft entered again in 1977. He received a letter from Keith MacKenzie, the Royal and Ancient secretary, informing him that he had provided no proof that his game had improved and so was unable to enter. Flitcroft challenged

MacKenzie to a match on the Old Course—MacKenzie did not accept.

The following year, Flitcroft entered the British Open as an American professional, Gene Pacecki ("as in 'paycheck,'" he later explained), and teed up at South Herts Golf Club outside London. But the organizers were onto him, and he was removed from the course after a handful of holes.

In 1983, having entered under the name of Gerald Hoppy, a professional from Switzerland, and sporting a false moustache and dyed hair, he teed up at Pleasington Golf Club in Lancashire. He played nine holes, scoring a comparatively respectable 63, before being found out and bundled off.

Seven years later, he entered the qualifier at Ormskirk, another Lancashire course, as James Beau Jolley, an American professional. He recorded a double bogey on the first hole, a bogey at the second, and said he was "looking at a par" on the third before a Royal and Ancient official challenged him. He asked if he could finish the hole but was shown no clemency. He was again taken from the course, and his £60 entry fee was not returned.

Flitcroft died on March 24, 2007, aged seventy-seven. Up

until his death, he maintained he was unfairly treated by the Royal and Ancient. "I never set out to belittle them," he said. "Golf's just a game and I tried my best. What did they need to get so uptight about?"

Fate

............•............

Just trust yourself.

A BEDRIDDEN HARVEY PENICK TO BEN CRENSHAW

BEFORE THE 1995 MASTERS

*No one knows what will happen in golf until it happens. All you can
do is work and suffer and wait for fate.*

BOBBY JONES, *THE GRAND SLAM*

As preparation for a major golf tournament goes, it certainly
wasn't ideal. Early on April 5, 1995, the day before The Masters
was due to start, Ben Crenshaw left Augusta National and flew
to Austin, Texas, to join fellow pro Tom Kite as a pallbearer

for his long-time coach, Harvey Penick, who had died at age ninety. It was a long and emotional day, and Crenshaw didn't return to Augusta until late that evening.

In addition to grieving for Penick, who had coached him since he was five, Crenshaw was worried about his game. He had missed cuts in three of his last four starts and hadn't broken 70 in two months. Most worryingly, he was ranked sixty-ninth on the PGA Tour in putting, normally the strongest part of his game. And at age forty-three, his time for major tournament wins was running out.

The following day, when Crenshaw teed off, people noted a calmness about him. He started with a 70 and followed it up with 67 and 69. At the end of the third day, he shared the leader-board at ten under par with Brian Henninger, with Davis Love III three shots behind. Also within spitting distance were Steve Elkington, Jay Haas, Scott Hoch, Curtis Strange, Greg Norman, and 24-year-old Phil Mickelson. Twenty-three players were within seven shots of the leader.

Crenshaw's smooth putting stroke had returned, and he had ridden his luck on several occasions. And in the final round, his good fortune continued. On the second hole, his drive flew into the trees, hit something hard, and bounded out.

"Another Harvey bounce," Crenshaw's wife, Julie, remarked to a friend. Crenshaw then birdied the hole.

Toward the end of the round, after much jockeying, three players were tied at twelve under—Crenshaw, Norman, and Love. On the thirteenth, Crenshaw holed out for a birdie and a one-shot lead. He missed a birdie putt on the fourteenth from 10 feet after an obedient bounce off a greenside mound.

Up ahead, Norman and Love, both of whom had been playing well, were having troubles. On the par-four seventeenth hole, Norman hit a 100-yard sand wedge about 15 yards left of the hole and three-putted. On the sixteenth, Love hit his ball right, just where he wanted it to go, and waited for it to feed down the hill to the flag—as balls have done at this hole ever since it was created. This time, however, the ball refused to budge, remaining steadfast on the edge of the precipice. Love three-putted and later would say, "Sometimes you wonder if things are meant to be." Love then birdied the seventeenth, and his 66 tied him with Crenshaw at thirteen under par.

On the sixteenth, Crenshaw hit a similar shot to Love's, and his ball ended up in the same part of the green. However, for some reason his ball wobbled, drifted left, and fed down to the hole. He sank the putt for a birdie and then birdied the seventeenth to lead by two with a hole to play. After he'd bogeyed the eighteenth for a 68 and a one-stroke victory, Crenshaw dropped his putter, bent over at the waist, buried his face in his hands, and cried. His long-time caddie, Carl Jackson, laid his big hands on Crenshaw's back to comfort him. The crowd rose and applauded, appreciating that Crenshaw's tears revealed not just his relief at winning the tournament, but his grief over Penick's death.

Love said afterward that fate had intervened. "I just had this feeling all week that this was going to happen," he said. "Either way, one of Harvey's boys was going to win."

"I believe in fate," Crenshaw said. "I don't know how it happened. I don't. It was kind of like I felt this hand on my shoulder, guiding me along. I had a fifteenth club in my bag."

Knowing Your Strengths

*The one stroke marks the difference between fame
and oblivion.*

SAMUEL PARISH, USGA TREASURER,

AMERICAN GOLFER, 1929

*The life of a professional athlete is precarious at best. Win and they
carry you to the clubhouse on their shoulders; lose and you pay the
caddies in the dark.*

GENE SARAZEN, *THIRTY YEARS OF CHAMPIONSHIP GOLF*

David Toms stood next to his ball on the fairway of the 492-yard final hole of the 2001 PGA, at the Atlanta Athletic Club, and gazed at the green. He had a five-wood in his hand and a one-stroke lead over Phil Mickelson. Neither player had won a major championship.

Toms had 213 yards to the pin, with water front and left. His ball lay in the first cut of rough but was 12 inches above his feet. The crowd looked at him expectantly, knowing that he faced the decision of a lifetime. Go for the green or lay up? Choices, choices . . .

Toms put away his wood and reached for his wedge. The crowd didn't like it. Some spectators rolled their eyes; others shook their heads. Don't players in the hunt at a tournament's death go for the green? Don't chickens lay up?

Toms proceeded to knock his ball down the fairway, leaving himself about 90 yards to the hole. "I hated to do it," he said later. "The crowd was over there oohing and ahhing and moaning like, 'You wimp.' I just had to put it out of my mind and hit two good shots and make a good putt."

Mickelson hit his second shot to about 10 yards. Toms then pitched his third shot to four yards.

Mickelson's putt stopped two inches short.

As Toms surveyed his putt, he knew that his reputation, as well as the outcome of the tournament, hinged on it. Miss it, and he would forever be known as the guy who laid up when a major was there to be won.

He settled over his putt . . . and he made it. If you're going to accept your limitations and lay up, do it right.

Keeping Your Eye on the Ball

............●............

Keep your head down and keep your eye on the ball. One shot at a time.

CADDIE EDDIE LOWERY TO FRANCIS OUIMET DURING

THE 1913 U.S. OPEN

During the two days preceding Francis's victory, and in the days
immediately afterward, the name Ouimet was used more than any
other word on the nation's telegraph and cable wires.

MARK FROST, *THE GREATEST GAME EVER PLAYED*

It is a simple black-and-white image that is embedded in the American sporting consciousness as deeply as that of Babe Ruth slugging one into the bleachers or Jesse Owens bursting out of the blocks at the 1936 Berlin Olympics. The photograph is of a slim 20-year-old amateur golfer, Francis Ouimet, walking down the fairway of The Country Club in Brookline, Massachusetts, during the 1913 U.S. Open, where he went head-to-head against famous British golfers Harry Vardon and Ted Ray.

In the picture, Ouimet, who was born to a humble family across the road from The Country Club, has a calmness about him. His tie is slightly askew, but his stride is purposeful and his gaze firm and focused on both the fairway and the task ahead. He holds a fairway wood lightly in his right hand. Alongside Ouimet is his ten-year-old caddie, Eddie Lowery, playing truant from school for the umpteenth time that month. The diminutive Lowery looks at the ground, his oversize shirt and Ouimet's outsize golf bag making him look even smaller.

Behind them, tramping the same turf, a group of onlookers talk excitedly to one another, not quite believing the events that were unfolding. Many of them had never seen golf before—it was relatively new to America—but most knew one thing: in its 18-year history, the U.S. Open had never been won by an amateur. The fact that a young local amateur, and a former caddie at that, was in the running was scarcely plausible.

Throughout the tournament, the expectation had been that Vardon and Ray, two giants of the game from the British Channel island of Jersey, would largely run a two-horse race. Vardon, the crisp shotmaker with the textbook swing and nerves of steel, had already won five British Opens, as well as the 1900 U.S. Open. Ray, a bull of a man whose powerful forearms and violent swing made him the game's longest hitter, had triumphed at the 1912 British Open at Muirfield, and he always seemed to be thereabouts in big tournaments. Ray "swayed his body, committed a number of minor crimes, and he used his enormous strength as much as he could," wrote Henry Leach, an English golf correspondent, in *American Golfer*.

It was thought that the pair perhaps would face some competition from John McDermott, who had won the two previous U.S. Opens, or from Jim Barnes or Macdonald Smith. Or maybe even from the young lad with the fast mouth and the fancy pants: Walter Hagen. But somehow, with one round to go, it was Francis Ouimet who was level with Ray and Vardon. Popular opinion had it that Ouimet would crumble under the weight of his partners' combined experience and his nation's expectations.

Ray and Vardon teed off well before Ouimet and finished even at 304 strokes for the four rounds. With nine holes to go, in tumbling rain, Ouimet remained level with the Englishmen and so had to play the final nine holes in par to join them in an 18-hole play-off. He started with a double bogey on the par-three tenth hole, smothering his tee shot, chipping on, and three-putting. He now trailed the Englishmen by two strokes with eight holes to play. The crowd began to disperse, some heading to the warmth of the clubhouse. The inexperienced challenger's game, as predicted, was beginning to unravel.

Regardless, as they walked to the eleventh tee, Lowery reminded Ouimet to keep his head down. Ouimet went on to par eleven and twelve, the latter from a fairway bunker. On thirteen, Lady Luck smiled. Ouimet chipped into the hole from the greenside rough for a birdie. The crowd erupted. Eyes became wide with expectation. Backs were slapped. Many of the nonbelievers who had decamped toward the clubhouse turned around.

Regulation pars at fourteen and fifteen left Ouimet with three holes to pick up the missing stroke. Against the odds, he holed a nasty 10-foot downhill putt on sixteen for his par. On seventeen, he drove right, away from the fairway bunker, and left himself about 150 yards to the pin. Using a jigger, he hit his ball 20 feet beyond the hole on the narrow green. The crowd surged to the green, and Ouimet and Lowery had to fight their way through.

Ouimet decided the line was a spot on the green eight inches outside the left edge of the hole. He narrowed his eyes, took a deep breath to settle his nerves, and sent the ball on its way. Initially, as the ball picked up speed down the slope, Ouimet thought he had overhit it. But the ball then took the break and clattered into the back of the hole.

As Bernard Darwin, golf writer for *The Times*, wrote later that evening, "The American crowd let loose and nearly dislocated its limbs in their joy." The pandemonium that erupted around the green could be heard in downtown Brookline. The amateur had drawn even! This was why the British had embraced this game for so long! Strangers embraced, hats were thrown skyward and the 10,000-strong crowd thronged to the final hole.

On eighteen, Ouimet drove well, then hit his second shot onto the fringe at the front of the green. He putted five feet past, then, displaying steady nerves far beyond his years, holed the return. The crowd roared for the third time in an hour. Ouimet had matched the Englishmen and would join the play-off the next day. The crowd rushed toward him and lifted him high on their shoulders. Eddie Lowery, momentarily afraid that he would be killed in the press, was also lifted into the air.

Darwin, who saw every shot of Ouimet's final round, wrote in *The Times*:

> After sober reflections I state my conviction that if I lived the length of a dozen lives I should never again be the spectator of such an amazing, thrilling and magnificent finish to an Open championship. Mr Ouimet's golf today was astonishing . . . All the most venerable of Bostonians appeared to have gone simultaneously mad, and for that matter, although my cheers were more restrained, I did not feel wholly sane myself. . . . It really seems impossible to believe that this young gentleman of twenty could hope to beat those two seasoned champions tomorrow. Even if he plays good enough golf, it seems almost too much to expect

that he should stand the strain. . . . It will be the greatest tie that has ever been played.

The next day, September 20, was gray and damp. The play-off started at 10 a.m., with Ouimet having successfully resisted calls for Lowery to be replaced by an older, more experienced caddie.

Little separated the three players through the first four holes. Ouimet hit out of bounds on five and took a bogey but birdied the eighth with a tap-in putt. After nine holes, all three players were on par: 38, dead even. Ouimet drew one ahead with a par on ten, then led by two shots after the twelfth. Vardon pulled one back on thirteen, and the trio all parred fourteen. Ray double-bogeyed fifteen while both Vardon and Ouimet secured their pars. Now it really was a two-horse race. Vardon and Ouimet both parred sixteen—the amateur led by one with two holes to play.

On seventeen, the scene of Ouimet's heroics the day before, Vardon went for distance off the tee and drove into the deep fairway bunker to the left of the dogleg. Today, this is known as "Vardon's bunker." Ouimet drove safely to the right. Vardon could do no better than a bogey, while Ouimet pitched to 16 feet . . . and holed the putt for a birdie.

Ouimet parred the last hole to shoot 72, beating Vardon by five and Ray by six. The world went beserk. Ouimet was lifted skyward, and someone handed him a horseshoe from the neighboring racetrack. A monumental grin split his face. A hat was passed around for Lowery, collecting $100—more money than he had ever seen before. Ray and Vardon offered their congratulations.

Ouimet's win represented a tipping point for American golf, moving the game from the preserve of the wealthy, aged, and/or British-born into the mainstream. Caddies, too, received a fillip—Ouimet, after all, had been one of them. The cheers from Brookline reverberated across the country. Throughout America, the wires clicked out the incredible story. The *New York Times* carried the saga on its front page, the first time golf had ever been featured so prominently.

Henry Leach, writing in the *New York Times*, summed up the feeling:

> You tell me that a child like this has beaten our Vardon and Ray for a real championship? When we can go for week-end golfing trips to Jupiter and Mars, I will perhaps believe that your little Ouimet

has won today. There will never be another like it. When we are old men little golfing children will ask us to tell them again the romantic story of the 20th of September in 1913.

Toughness

............•............

If you ever feel sorry for somebody on a golf course, you better go home. If you don't kill them, they'll kill you.

SEVE BALLESTEROS, *SEVE: THE YOUNG CHAMPION*

Asking Raymond Floyd to scramble was like throwing a rabbit into a briar patch.

RON GREEN, *GOLF'S GREATEST EIGHTEEN*

When US Ryder Cup captain Tom Watson was asked which traits he sought in his two captain's choices on the eve of the 1993 tournament at The Belfry, near Birmingham in the English

117

Midlands, he answered, "Heart and guts." That was why one of his choices had been 50-year-old Raymond Floyd.

Floyd, partnering Fred Couples, lost his opening foursomes match, 4 and 3, to Nick Faldo and Colin Montgomerie, but then peeled off three wins over the remaining two days—a foursomes and a four-ball match partnering Payne Stewart, and then a triumph over Spaniard Jose Maria Olazabal in the singles. The United States won the Ryder Cup, 15 points to 13. If Watson had had to name a hero in his team, it would have been Floyd.

Raymond Floyd made a career out of performing against the odds, and producing the unexpected. In 1992, he became the first person to win on the PGA Tour and the Senior PGA Tour in the same year. His regular-tour victory, in the Doral Ryder Open, meant that he had won tournaments in four different decades. Floyd had an ungainly swing, labored and jerky, but more than made up for it by possessing the hide of a rhinoceros. He had a razor-sharp short game and a willingness to scrap until the final putt dropped.

Most important, from the moment he picked up a club, Floyd was happy to scramble. If he was behind, he fought tooth and nail. If he was ahead, he did everything to stay there. If he had to make a putt, he usually did—it seemed that the higher the stakes, the greater the chance he'd hole it. Aside from Sam Snead, Floyd performed at the top of his craft for longer than perhaps any other great player.

It all started, from a professional point of view, on March 17, 1963, when Floyd shot a final-round score of 69 to win the St Petersburg Open in Florida, scrambling successfully all day. Remarkably, he was only twenty years, six months, and three days old and had only been on the tour for four months. After this early success, Floyd achieved little over the next six years. Then, in 1969, he won three tournaments, including the PGA at the NCR Country Club in Dayton, Ohio.

Another six-year drought followed, which he broke spectacularly in 1976 when he won The Masters, shooting 65, 66, 70, and 70, beating runner-up Ben Crenshaw by eight shots. Tom Weiskopf described Floyd's score of 271, which matched Jack Nicklaus's record-winning score of 1965, as "one of the greatest feats this game has seen."

In 1982, Floyd won another PGA, at a hot and steamy Southern Hills in Oklahoma, opening with a 63, a round he described as "probably the best round of golf I've ever played, anywhere." From holes seven to fifteen, he had nine straight threes. His 69 on the Friday set a record for the lowest halfway score in the tournament, his 68 on the Saturday set a record for 54 holes, and his total of 272 was the second-lowest score ever to win the PGA.

At the 1986 U.S. Open at Shinnecock Hills in Southampton, Long Island, Floyd continued to rewrite the record books. Few would have seen it coming. In his 22 previous starts, Floyd's best finish had been sixth, and he had made the top ten only twice. On top of that, he was about to turn forty-four, and no one had ever won the U.S. Open at that age.

The first day of the tournament was cold and wet—good weather for scrambling. Floyd shot 75, which put him in the hunt, and he followed up with a 68 and a 70. In the final round, confronting a packed leader board, he closed with a 66 to win by two. He had remained gimlet-eyed and poker-faced throughout, quietly doing the job that had to be done.

"Raymond had that look in his eyes," Lanny Wadkins said later. "When he gets that look, he's hard to handle. Raymond's a good door slammer."

Despite the fact that he was now the oldest-ever U.S. Open winner, Floyd wasn't done. In 1992, aged forty-nine, he came in second at The Masters to Fred Couples, and he then won the Doral Ryder Open. That's what got him his start in Tom Watson's "heart and guts" Ryder Cup team.

Claude Harmon, winner of the 1948 Masters, was fond of saying, "The game's not called pretty, it's called golf"—the winner is not the player with the sweetest swing, but the player with the lowest score. Raymond Floyd would tip his hat to that.

Tenacity

·············●·············

Victory is everything. You can spend the money,
but you can never spend the memories.

KEN VENTURI, COLONIAL NATIONAL INVITATION,

CBS-TV, 1983

Mr Ken, I don't mind telling you, but when you picked my name out
of the hat, I wasn't too pleased. I wanted to get one of the favorites,
but I want to tell you something. You're the damndest golfer I ever
saw in my life.

CADDIE WILLIAM WARD TO KEN VENTURI AFTER

THE 1964 U.S. OPEN

The 1964 U.S. Open was held in a cauldron of heat at the Congressional Country Club in Washington, DC. The temperature was over 100 degrees, the humidity was stultifying, and the air was so still it shimmered. On top of all that, Congressional was the longest course ever selected in the tournament's 69 years.

American Ken Venturi didn't go into the tournament with high hopes. Two years earlier, he had pinched a nerve in his back, which almost paralyzed the right side of his body. His golf game suffered terribly, and he had found himself in the doldrums for three years, racked by self-doubt. By 1964, he was 94th on the money list and practically broke. He had resorted to asking friends for sponsor exemptions to tournaments— even the shirt company that sponsored him had decided its money was better spent elsewhere.

This was all a far cry from Venturi's early golf career, when he'd been a whisker away from winning The Masters, not once but three times—in 1956 (as an amateur, he came in second by a shot after leading by four going into the final round), 1958 (tied for fourth), and 1960 (second by a shot after Arnold Palmer birdied the final two holes). Nonetheless, in 1964, Venturi successfully qualified for the U.S. Open for the first time in five years. At the time, he carried with him a letter written by San Francisco priest Father Kevin Murray, telling Venturi that the pain and the turmoil he had undergone would be the bedrock of a new character, that the new Ken Venturi would possess a strength of spirit that would not yield.

Venturi's opening round of 72 left him four shots behind Arnold Palmer. A second-round 70 kept him in the hunt, and a 66 in the third round propelled him to within two shots of leader Tommy Jacobs. But Venturi, a native of mild-weathered San Francisco, was not used to the heat, and it started to show late in the third round, when his body began to shake with heat exhaustion. "I don't think I'll make it, Ray," he said to playing partner Raymond Floyd on the seventeenth tee. He subsequently missed short putts on that hole and the eighteenth.

In 1964, the final two rounds of the U.S. Open were still being played on the same day (it was the last year that this would happen), and players were given less than an hour off between them. After he finished his third round, Venturi was taken from the eighteenth green to the clubhouse, where he lay down on the floor. Dr John Everett, Congressional member and chairman of the tournament's medical committee, fed him iced tea and salt tablets and suggested they go straight to the hospital. A return to the course, Everett warned, could be fatal.

But Venturi, who hadn't been in a position to win a tournament for ages, wouldn't hear of it. Accompanied by Everett, who carried a supply of cold towels, he slowly made his way to the first tee to resume the battle. "All I tried to do was what it always takes to win the U.S. Open: fairways and greens, fairways and greens," he recalled in his 2004 autobiography, *Getting Up and Down*.

Venturi played the first few holes in a dream-like state, moving like a sleepwalker and retreating to the shade whenever possible. Several times, he thought he would pass out. Somehow, he parred eight of the first nine holes and was tied with Jacobs at the turn. Despite his exhaustion, he continued to play steady golf, scoring pars and the odd birdie. With five holes to go, he complained to USGA head Joe Dey that he could hardly walk. The crowd urged him on.

On the 211-yard sixteenth hole, Venturi hit a one-iron shot that landed on the front of the green and bounded forward to hit the flag stick. Then, on the eighteenth, leading by four shots, he hit his five-iron approach into the greenside bunker.

"Hold your head high, Ken," Dey told him as they approached the green.

Venturi got up and down from the bunker, holing a 10-foot putt for par, and promptly broke down. His playing partner, Floyd, pulled the ball out of the hole for him and also began to cry. Venturi had shot a final round 70 for a total of 278.

When Venturi handed Floyd's card to him in the scorer's tent, there were no numbers on it. "To this day, I can't tell you about a single shot he hit," Venturi wrote in his book.

Concentration

...........●............

You couldn't tell whether Cotton was in the right or left side of the
fairway because his ball was so close to the middle.

BOB TOSKI, *GOLF DIGEST*, 1983

The only problem in major golf is, as ever, "how to score," for nearly
all the players setting out on the circuits can hit the ball.
That is no problem.

HENRY COTTON

In 1920—not long after the end of World War I—George
Cotton, the owner of a large and successful British iron

foundry, took his two young sons, Henry and Leslie, to see J.H. Taylor, winner of five British Opens. He was keen to get the great golfer's opinion on whether either of his sons possessed a game good enough to develop.

Taylor put the boys through their paces and announced that he thought 13-year-old Henry "would be the better player as he had more determination and more power of concentration." Notably, he didn't mention anything about natural ability, but he clearly felt the boy's other attributes could take him places.

Taylor's words were prophetic. In 1934, at Royal St. George's on the Kent coast, Henry Cotton opened the tournament with rounds of 67 and 65, setting a 36-hole total of 132 that would not be beaten until Nick Faldo shot 130 at Muirfield in 1992.

The golfing world was astounded at Cotton's two rounds. Sporting-goods manufacturer Dunlop would later name a ball after Cotton's second round—the famous Dunlop 65—which for decades would be the bestselling golf ball in Britain.

Cotton's opening rounds gave him a nine-shot lead. Americans had won the previous ten British Opens, so Cotton's first thirty-six holes led to an outpouring of national fervor. People piled into Royal St. George's to witness the final day's play, thirty-six holes, and their countryman's inevitable crowning.

A third-round 72 in the morning was relatively humdrum but increased Cotton's lead to ten shots over the dogged Macdonald Smith.

The fourth round, that afternoon, was delayed due to crowd-control problems. Cotton had to wait in a tent for calm to be restored. His nerves gnawed at him. He had eaten his lunch too quickly, and the resulting stomach cramps seemed to accentuate the burden of expectation.

He completed a very un-Cotton-like front nine—40 strokes—and was saved only by his putting. All of a sudden, there was a possibility that he might not win. Although his golf wasn't much better on the second nine, 39, his four-round total of 283 was good enough to win the title by five strokes and equal Gene Sarazen's record low score of 283, shot at nearby Prince's two years earlier. Sid Brews came second, Alf Padgham third, while Macdonald Smith and Frenchman Marcel Dallemagne were tied for fourth.

Cotton became a national hero, his win refuting all suggestions that the Americans had an eternal stranglehold on the country's national championship. Cotton fitted the bill nicely: he was well dressed, self-possessed, and articulate. Later, as a coach and mentor to aspiring players and professionals, he would stress the importance of manners, clean fingernails, polished shoes, and letter writing. He would also work hard to promote the status of professional golfers.

Cotton was a great thinker of the game. Walter Hagen called him "Concentration Henry." In his early years, he spent hours working with clubs and tinkering with his swing, as well as analyzing the swings of others. He decided that rather than try to copy someone else's swing, he should simply develop his own. He put great emphasis on the value of strong hands and wrists and spent hours squeezing a rubber ball and hitting an old tire with a club. Cotton's love of practice eventually led to his right shoulder ending up lower than his left.

His long hours of practice gave him the ability to generate enormous power with his drives from only a three-quarter swing. His driving was unerringly straight—a huge advantage, especially on European courses lined by heavy rough. He enjoyed showing students that he could play a long, straight shot with both feet pointing at the target, and then he would do the same with his feet pointing away from the target. Gene

Sarazen said, "There are few golfers who know as much as Cotton does about the dynamics of the golf swing and who strike the ball as correctly and compactly."

Cotton was prepared to travel widely to learn. Aged twenty-one, impressed by the American dominance of his national championship, he traveled to the United States to experience the toughest and most competitive tournaments. The following year, he played in Argentina. This experience served him well in Europe, where he won eleven Open titles including the national championships of Belgium, Germany, France, and Italy.

But his great love was the British Open, which he won three times. And in each win, his concentration and his determination allowed him to pull off one fine round to draw away from the field.

His second win, at Carnoustie in 1937, may well have been better than his first. The opposition was certainly better; the American Ryder Cup players had remained in Britain to try their hands at the Open Championship. These included Sam Snead, Byron Nelson, Gene Sarazen, and Walter Hagen. Bernard Darwin, writing in *The Times*, said the Americans seemed "to do 72s like clockwork" and predicted a Snead win.

Cotton started with 74 and 72 and found himself four shots behind Reg Whitcombe. The weather on the last day—when two rounds were played—was terrible, ranging from heavy showers to biblical downpours. Cotton shot 73 in the morning and drew to within three strokes of Whitcombe. The final round was almost abandoned due to the weather, but Cotton was able to keep his steely determination and concentration intact, his 71 giving him a two-stroke victory over Whitcombe, who could only manage 76. Given the conditions, it was possibly the finest round of golf Cotton ever played.

Many were surprised that Cotton did not travel to America during his heyday. Gene Sarazen ventured: "I think he might have passed up a few of those Czechoslovak Opens in favor of visiting the States when he was at his peak."

World War II robbed Cotton of several chances to add to his Open haul, but he would have one more triumph, in 1948 at Muirfield. A first-round 71 put him two strokes off the lead. The next day, watched by King George VI—an avid golfer— Cotton broke the course record with a 66, which gave him the lead by four shots. In the third round, Sam King caught him momentarily, but Cotton produced two birdies and entered the final round with a two-shot lead. A 72 in the afternoon sealed the win by five shots over Fred Daly, with four players a shot further back, including Australia's Norman von Nida and Argentina's Roberto de Vicenzo.

In 1987, just before he died, Henry Cotton learned he would become the first player to be knighted for services to golf.

Preparation

In effect Ben basically taught himself an entirely different sort of game. In my mind it was his most amazing feat ever.

JOHN DERR, CBS BROADCASTER, ON BEN HOGAN'S PREPARATION FOR THE 1953 BRITISH OPEN, IN *BEN HOGAN: THE AUTHORISED BIOGRAPHY,* BY JAMES DODSON

A man who puts his ball there won't be contending anyway.

BEN HOGAN, ON WHY HE DIDN'T PRACTICE SHOTS FROM CARNOUSTIE'S HEATHER AND GORSE, IN *BEN HOGAN: THE AUTHORISED BIOGRAPHY*

Anyone who happened to venture out onto the bleak and windswept Scottish links of Carnoustie in late June 1953, a week before the British Open was to commence, may well have noticed a small, straight-backed man walking the holes in reverse order. The man walked around greens and adjacent bunkers and examined both with the attentiveness of a surgeon. Occasionally, he would stop, drag on a cigarette, and stare into the distance. Halfway down each fairway, he would stop and squint at the green, then turn 180 degrees and look at the tee. He would repeat this exercise from various angles on each fairway.

He peered into fairway bunkers, occasionally sifting sand through his fingers, and walked to the side of each fairway to examine the rough, as if searching for something. He paid particular attention to a small bunker toward the left-hand side of the fairway on the par-five sixth hole, and the 8-yard strip of land that separated it from the out-of-bounds fence.

To the uninitiated, the identity of the man would likely have been a mystery. To those who followed golf across the Atlantic, the checkered wool cap and immaculately creased trousers would have given a clue to who he was.

Ben Hogan played in only one British Open, at Carnoustie

135

in 1953, and he won it. He was forty at the time and at the top of his game, having won four U.S. Opens, two PGAs, and two Masters. He had been needled continually by his colleagues about having a go at the British Open and had decided to follow the lead of compatriots Walter Hagen, Bobby Jones, Gene Sarazen, and Sam Snead.

Like most things Hogan did, he prepared assiduously, leaving as little as possible to chance. He saw the winning of golf tournaments as an exercise in practicality and planning, like a mathematician working out a quadratic equation. If you can hit the ball where you want, the next thing is to work out where to hit it—learn the safe routes, avoid the dangers, reduce the variables. To Hogan, winning was simply the process of finding the safest way to shoot the lowest score.

Aside from practicing at Carnoustie for the better part of two weeks, often hitting three balls from each tee, Hogan also practiced at nearby Panmure. He had to learn to play from tight lies and work out the distances he could hit the smaller British ball, which behaved differently in the wind.

Hogan employed as his caddie Cecil Timms, a fine local amateur, and told him that he would not be required to select clubs nor read greens, a directive that bemused Timms. In fact,

Hogan said little to Timms the entire week of the championship, apart from asking him for cigarettes and telling him to leave his bag of sweets alone, after Timms had helped himself to them on the first day.

Many of the great American players were not at Carnoustie that year, but the field included defending champion Bobby Locke, Australian Peter Thomson, Argentine Roberto de Vicenzo, Americans Lloyd Mangrum and the amateur Frank Stranahan (who would not turn professional until the following year), former British Open winner Max Faulkner, Welshman Dai Rees, and the fine Irish players Christy O'Connor and Fred Daly.

Despite the fact that he was the current U.S. Open and Masters champion, Hogan still had to prequalify for the tournament. He shot 70 and 75 and did so easily.

On the first hole of the championship, in front of a huge crowd, Hogan split the fairway with a three-wood. He went on to play solid, unspectacular golf that first day—his 73 placed him three strokes behind Stranahan and one behind de Vicenzo, Locke, Thomson, and Rees. He did, however, get angry with himself for finding two bunkers. And although Hogan's long game was as solid as ever, his putting was beginning to fail him in his twenty-first year of top-level golf. Occasionally, Timms covered his eyes when Hogan was putting and sighed loudly when he missed. Hogan rebuked him: "If it's so damned hard to watch just stand there, Timmy, and look away. Don't make such a show out of it. For God's sake, calm down."

Hogan shot 71 in the second round, again missing several midlength birdie putts. At the halfway mark of the tournament, he was two strokes shy of Rees and Scotland's Eric Brown. On the final day, with thirty-six holes to play, Hogan woke with a cold and was given a shot of penicillin before his midmorning tee time. Despite a three-putt on the seventeenth, he shot 70 and, with a round to go, was tied for the lead with de Vicenzo.

Between rounds, de Vicenzo sat in his hotel room and wept, convinced his putting was not good enough to win. Hogan, meanwhile, had a sandwich and collected his thoughts. Timms, far more nervous than Hogan, sat with the golfer's wife, Valerie, in a different room.

Hogan started his final round with four pars. He got a bad break on the fifth when his ball rolled off the green and stopped on a patch of sandy rough near the edge of a bunker. He took a full four minutes to decide how to play the shot, eventually opting to nip a nine-iron off the bare lie. His ball bounded twice on the green, lost speed on a bank, and hit the back of the cup, bouncing into the air before falling in. The unexpected birdie put Hogan ahead in the tournament for the first time.

Hogan famously drove left of the bunker on the sixth, onto the eight-yard strip of ground now called Hogan's Alley, and then birdied the hole. He bagged another birdie on the par-three thirteenth and later confided that he knew then that the tournament was his. He birdied the final hole (then a par five) and won by four shots.

No one seemed surprised, certainly not the player himself, that Hogan's scores had improved round by round, from 73 to 71, 70, and 68. They had a certain Hoganesque pattern about them. His final-round 68 was a new course record for Carnoustie, and his 72-hole score of 282 was a record score for a Carnoustie Open, bettering Henry Cotton's pre–World War II score of 290. Extraordinarily, Hogan had not missed a single fairway during the tournament.

The win, and the way in which he achieved it, burnished Hogan's already glowing reputation as the world's best golfer. That year, Hogan won three majors by a total of fifteen strokes:

four in the British Open, five in The Masters, and six in the U.S. Open (the fourth major, the PGA, clashed with the British Open).

Some suspected that Hogan's fastidious preparation for the 1953 British Open meant that it would be his one and only tilt at the title, win or lose. They were right. Hogan never returned.

Conviction

............●............

*So bewilderingly picturesque that it seems to have been the
crystallization of the dream of an artist who has been drinking gin
and sobering up on absinthe.*

O.B. KEELER ON CYPRESS POINT, *AMERICAN GOLFER*, 1929

There should be a sufficient number of heroic carries from the tee.

DR. ALISTER MACKENZIE'S EIGHTH PRINCIPLE OF GOLF COURSE
DESIGN, *GOLF ARCHITECTURE*

Arguably, no golf shot has had a greater impact on golf course
architecture than the one hit over 230 yards of swirling ocean

by former US women's amateur champion Marion Hollins near the Californian town of Monterey in 1926.

In the mid-1920s, Hollins, a native of Long Island who grew up playing a multitude of sports, traveled to California for a holiday with her family. There, she met Samuel Morse, the builder and owner of Pebble Beach Golf Links. Morse was impressed with Hollins's sporting pedigree and signed her up as athletic director at his club. He then challenged her to develop a first-class private golf club, to be called Cypress Point, on a stretch of wild duneland and rocky promontories between the towns of Carmel and Pacific Grove. Course architect Seth Raynor had initially been given the job but had died of pneumonia in 1926 having only drawn up preliminary plans.

It so happened that around the time of Hollins's appointment, renowned British golf course architect Dr. Alister MacKenzie arrived in the United States during a world trip that had included stops in Australia and New Zealand. He met Morse and Hollins and was subsequently employed to finish designing Cypress Point, falling in love with the land presented to him.

MacKenzie agreed with Raynor's proposition that there was a significant problem with the concept of making the sixteenth hole a 230-yard par three, involving a drive over the ocean to a landing area on a mighty point of land reaching into the Pacific. The proposed hole certainly met one of MacKenzie's thirteen principles of golf design, the heroic carry, but this particular challenge, he reasoned, was simply beyond most golfers.

MacKenzie resigned himself to making the hole a par four, suggesting that players aim left for their drive, a much shorter carry, and then pitch onto the green. He told Hollins his decision as they stood on the tee and surveyed the scene. Hollins's reaction was to tee up a ball and nail it with her brassie—a hickory-shafted two-wood—to the planned site of the green.

MacKenzie's response, once he had recovered, was something along the lines of: "Well, that's that then."

"To give honor where it is due," MacKenzie wrote in his book *The Spirit of St. Andrews*, "I must say that, except for minor details in construction, I was in no way responsible for the hole. It was largely due to the vision of Miss Marion Hollins."

The sixteenth at Cypress Point, most definitely a par three, is now arguably the most famous hole in golf. It is certainly the most photogenic, and possibly the most beloved hole in the world. Anyone who stands on the tee and looks at the roiling surf and the green in the distance, the barking of sea otters in their ears, and wonders how they will possibly reach the green in one has Marion Hollins to thank.

Meeting Challenges

............●............

*I thought the course treated me rather cruelly. I'm not an obnoxious
guy. I don't throw clubs. I'm nice to galleries. I don't deserve some of
the things Pebble Beach did to me.*

BILL ISRAELSON, MINNESOTA PROFESSIONAL,
AFTER SHOOTING 83 IN THE FINAL ROUND OF 1982
U.S. OPEN, *SAN FRANCISCO EXAMINER*

Pebble Beach is Alcatraz with grass.

BOB HOPE AT THE BING CROSBY NATIONAL PRO-AM, 1952

Every ten years or so, the U.S. Open is held at Pebble Beach
on California's Monterey Peninsula. These tournaments always

seem to produce a well-known and worthy winner—Jack Nicklaus won in 1972 and Tom Watson in 1982. But neither win was more dramatic, or more hard-fought, than Tom Kite's in 1992.

The first three days of the 1992 championship were benign—blue sky, no wind—and the players responded with champagne golf. On the first day, twenty-nine players broke par, led by Gil Morgan's 66, one better than two-time champion Curtis Strange. Andy Dillard shot 68 after birdying the first six holes. Morgan managed a 69 in the second round and led Dillard by three strokes after thirty-six holes. Raymond Floyd and Australia's Wayne Grady were tied for third at four under par.

Meanwhile, one of golf's journeymen, Tom Kite, shot a par 72 to join eleven others at one under par, eight shots behind Morgan. Although Kite had had a glittering career, earning bags of prize money and plenty of wins on the US tour, a major had eluded him. At age forty-two, time was not on his side.

In the third round, Morgan made history on the third hole when a 30-foot birdie putt took him to ten under par—he was the first person to do this in the tournament's history. Birdies at both the sixth and seventh holes took him to twelve under par, a lead of seven shots. But it didn't last; by the end of the round, Morgan had dropped several shots and returned to the pack, leading by one over Ian Woosnam, Mark Brooks, and Kite.

Overnight, a low-pressure system moved over the Californian coast and the wind was blowing hard when the first players arrived on the course for the closing round. By the time the last groups had teed off, the wind was gusting at 43 miles an hour. Not long after the leaders had teed off, Colin Montgomerie finished his final round in 70. Due to the change in weather, his total of 288—par—was looking better by the minute. Jack Nicklaus, who knew a thing or two about Pebble Beach, declared from the ABC-TV broadcast booth that Montgomerie's score would be good enough to win.

The wind dried out the small greens, making them faster. Putting became a lottery. That day, only five players broke or matched par. Twenty failed to break 80, including Scott Simpson (who shot 88), Mark Brooks, Davis Love III, Mark Calcavecchia, and Paul Azinger.

It was a day for patience, discipline, and courage. Kite had all three, as well as a bit of luck. He missed the 106-yard seventh hole, then chipped in for a two. He holed a 33-foot putt on the twelfth green, then birdied the long fourteenth, aiming for the

147

rough to the left of the green rather than aiming for the flag and running through into trouble. His final round of 72 gave him a two-stroke win over Jeff Sluman, with Montgomerie another stroke back.

"I guess if you can only win one major championship, it would be the U.S. Open," Kite said afterward. "And if you had to pick a golf course to win it, Pebble Beach is not a bad place to have it."

After he had won, Kite had another engagement but dearly wanted Harvey Penick, who had coached him as a young, aspiring golfer and who was now in his late eighties, to see the trophy. Kite's wife, Christy, took the trophy to Austin, Texas, and approached Penick with the words, "I have something here you own a part of."

Fighting Fear

············●············

When a putter is waiting his turn to hole out a putt of one or two feet in length on which the match hangs at the last hole, it is of vital importance that he think of nothing. At this supreme moment he ought studiously to fill his mind with vacancy. He must not even allow himself the consolation of religion.

SIR WALTER SIMPSON, *THE ART OF GOLF*

Once you've had 'em, you've got 'em.

HENRY LONGHURST ON THE PUTTING YIPS

There is no more horrifying description of the putting yips than that provided by Tommy Armour, winner of the 1927 U.S. Open, the 1930 PGA, and the 1931 British Open. The yips, Armour said in his book *The ABCs of Golf*, is "that ghastly time when, with the first movement of the putter, the golfer blacks out, loses sight of the ball, and hasn't the remotest idea of what to do with the putter, or, occasionally, that he is holding a putter at all."

The yips—also known as the twitches, the jitters, and the jerks—have sunk their claws into players of the caliber of Ben Hogan, Sam Snead, Harry Vardon, "Wild Bill" Mehlhorn, and Peter Alliss. Some yippers leave putts short, others fire them past the hole. Some can't even take the putter back.

In 1927, Mehlhorn, playing in a tournament with Bobby Jones, yipped on a three-foot putt and sent the ball scooting past the hole into a greenside bunker. He then had to endure perhaps the ultimate ignominy in golf—swapping a putter for a sand wedge.

No one has had the yips worse than German Bernhard Langer, and no one has worked harder to work out how to control them, nor has had better results. When Langer, the son of a Czechoslovakian war refugee, first arrived on the

European tour in 1974, aged eighteen, he was an instinctively wonderful putter. Then, during a match between the Continent and Britain, the yips set in. Langer found he was unable to hole short putts. Spectators turned away lest they be affected—all golfers know that yips are contagious.

Langer later described them as "an uncontrollable movement of the muscles. It can go anywhere from a twitch, to a freeze where you can't move at all, to a sudden explosion."

Perhaps to his relief, Langer left golf to do military service for eighteen months. When he returned to the game, he tried new putters but eventually settled for something completely different. He hunched over his putter like Quasimodo, holding the shaft against his left forearm with his right hand, while his left hand grasped the shaft farther down. It was ungainly, and people laughed, but it was effective. As happens with all good ideas, other sufferers of the yips have since adopted Langer's technique.

Occasionally, Langer's yips returned—such as during the 1982 European PGA Championship at Hillside Golf Club in northern England, when he four-putted the sixteenth green in the final round—but he refused to be beaten. Through sheer willpower and Teutonic tenacity, he won the 1985 Masters on the world's most treacherous greens, at Augusta National, shooting 68 in each of the final two rounds to win by two shots over Curtis Strange, Seve Ballesteros, and Raymond Floyd.

To prove it was no fluke, he did it again at the 1993 Masters.

Grinding It Out

To match par in this course you've got be luckier than a dog with two tails.

SAM SNEAD ON WINGED FOOT GOLF CLUB

On Tuesday night, some kids got out on the golf course and drove a car over the first green. I got out there on Wednesday morning and couldn't see any damage, the green was so firm it didn't even make a scratch.

SANDY TATUM, USGA PRESIDENT, ON THE WINGED FOOT GREENS, 1974

Even the most hardened golfers were surprised at the brutal conditions confronting them at Winged Foot Golf Club, at Mamaroneck outside New York City, when they arrived for the 1974 U.S. Open. The fairways were narrower than normal, the rough higher than usual, and the sloping greens were as hard as quartz.

The seasoned players muttered that an Open course hadn't been set up so hard since the 1955 event at Olympic in San Francisco, which had waist-high rough and where Jack Fleck won in a play-off over Ben Hogan after both had shot 287. Some suspected the course set-up was in response to Johnny Miller's extraordinary 63, which had helped him win the previous year's U.S. Open at Oakmont in Pennsylvania.

Jack Nicklaus described the course as "merciless." One writer dubbed the tournament "Massacre at Winged Foot." USGA President Sandy Tatum's response to the criticism was pointed: "We're not trying to humiliate the greatest players in the world. We're trying to identify them."

Among the field was Hale Irwin, in his seventh year on the PGA Tour. A former football player, Irwin's career had been far from spectacular, with only two tour wins. But he was known as a tough competitor who often performed well in difficult circumstances.

Irwin described the practice rounds at Winged Foot as "brutal" and the course as the "hardest I have ever played, not only before but since." But he was not concerned. Everyone, he reasoned, was going to make bogeys, so the key was to make as few bogeys as possible. Par on any hole would be a good score. He had to be patient and steady and needed to keep his emotions under control.

Fewer than one player in six broke 75 on the first day—Irwin's first-round 73 saw him trailing Gary Player by three strokes. A second-round 70 had Irwin tied with a triumvirate well known for being comfortable in a scrap—Player, Arnold Palmer, and Raymond Floyd. A third-round 71 had Irwin one behind Tom Watson and level with Palmer.

In the final round, Irwin played steady golf for the first eight holes, then received manna from heaven: a rare birdie on nine. When he eventually stood on the tee of the 437-yard seventeenth hole, the tournament was on a knife's edge. Leader-boards were not prevalent in those days, so Irwin assumed he was leading, but he didn't know whether it was by one shot or two. He drove into the rough and hacked the ball out onto the fairway, over 100 yards from the pin. He then hit a wedge to three yards. He said later, "I felt I had to make this putt to keep the lead or at least be tied. It wasn't an easy putt, but I made it, and that was just the symbol of how I played that week. I kept grinding it out."

Irwin had a two-shot lead with a hole to go. He drove down the middle of the eighteenth fairway and hit a two-iron to the green followed by two putts to win by two. His seven-over-par total was the second-highest in a U.S. Open since World War II. Apart from Irwin and runner-up Forrest Fezler, everyone else in the field had double figures over par.

Many golfers play well week to week in the minor tournaments but fade away when conditions are tougher or when the pressure increases. Others, far smaller in number, seem to play better when conditions require players to grind away. Hale Irwin is one of them.

In a career that spanned 27 years, Irwin recorded 28 wins. Remarkably, three of those were in the U.S. Open, the tournament that most players believe is the hardest to win.

Irwin, who learned to play golf on a municipal course in Kansas with sandy greens, has said:

I've always felt that tenacity was something
I've had. That would apply to most things that
I have tried to do. Scaling a brick wall may be
impossible, but if you can find a few handholds,
maybe you can still do it. You can call it guts. You
can call it confidence. You can call it experience.
I've never abandoned my beliefs. Some things are
improbable, but I've never thought many things
are impossible.

Irwin won his second U.S. Open in 1979 at The Inverness
Club in Toledo, Ohio, another course with a reputation for
denying good scores in the event. He shot 74, 68, 67, and 75
to win by two shots over Gary Player and Jerry Pate. He had
limped home, dropping four shots in the final nine holes and
finishing at level par: 284.

In 1990, the U.S. Open returned to Medinah in Chicago.
Irwin, now aged forty-five and coming off three winless years,
was only playing because he received an exemption from the
PGA. After three rounds, he was tied for twentieth, four behind
the leader, tour journeyman Mike Donald. He played the first
nine of the final round in par but was losing ground as those

behind him recorded birdies. Irwin then played the final eight holes in five under par.

On the last hole, he found himself nearly 60 feet from the pin. He holed the putt for a birdie and then ran full circle around the green, punching the air and high-fiving the fans. After waiting two hours, he found out that his score was good enough to get into a play-off—Donald had bogeyed the sixteenth hole.

In the play-off, the Irwin script was being followed yet again. Donald held a two-shot advantage with six holes to play. Irwin recalled of the final few holes:

> It was getting difficult for me to believe it could still happen, but I told myself to keep going, keep going. You never know what can happen, that's what I kept telling myself, because a two-shot lead can be overtaken in one hole. Just keep hitting the shots. Think only of the next shot because it's the most important one you can play.

On the 437-yard sixteenth hole, Irwin found himself with a two-iron in his hand, facing a 207-yard uphill shot, into the wind, that also required a draw around some trees. He hit his ball to six-and-a-half feet and made the putt.

Donald bogeyed the last hole, driving into the rough, to push the play-off into sudden death. On the first of these holes, Irwin hit to 10 feet and made the putt for birdie. At forty-five, he was the oldest champion in U.S. Open history.

Irwin owes his success to hard work, belief, and the ability to keep grinding away at the task in front of him: "The game has its own humility. One time you think you are on top of the game, and the next day it's got you by the throat. You have to perform with your heart and soul."

Little Things Matter

............●............

The man who can putt is a match for anyone.

WILLIE PARK JUNIOR, SCOTTISH PROFESSIONAL

If you couldn't putt, Billy, you'd be selling hot dogs outside the ropes.

BEN HOGAN TO BILLY CASPER, WINGED FOOT, 1959

Golf has produced many great putters—Walter Travis, Bobby Locke, Tom Watson, Bob Charles, Isao Aoki, Ben Crenshaw, Tiger Woods.

None has been better than William Earl "Billy" Casper.

During his peak in the 1960s, Casper's long game relied on a controlled fade—often the staple diet of champions—and he was not overly long. He rarely went for par fives in two and usually played to the fat of the green, rather than the pin. This approach, and his rather drab line in clothing, prompted Tommy Bolt to say once: "Watching Casper play golf is like watching a Rolls Royce drive up to the Waldorf Astoria and no one gets out."

But Casper had one thing going for him—he could putt the lights out.

It was largely Casper's putting that enabled him to win 56 tournaments around the world, including two U.S. Opens, a Masters, two Brazilian Opens, the Italian Open, the Mexican Open, and the Havana Invitational.

He also won several prestigious tournaments multiple times, including four Western Opens, four Hartford Opens, two Colonial Invitationals, two Doral Opens, and two Los Angeles Opens. He played on eight US Ryder Cup teams and was a five-time winner of the Vardon Trophy for the lowest stroke average on the PGA Tour.

Talk in the 1960s was of The Big Three, referring to Arnold Palmer, Gary Player, and Jack Nicklaus. Such was Casper's record during this decade, it could easily have been The Big Four.

Casper used the old-fashioned "pop" putting technique, holding the putter square through the takeaway and then hitting with a short, firm stroke. He held his putter close to his body, his hands almost touching his legs when addressing the ball. His left hand would often brush his left thigh on his follow-through. It was a wristy style that he developed in his youth on the slow, uneven greens on municipal greens in San Diego and that is very different from the smooth, long putting strokes of today's professionals, who play on better surfaces.

Casper's putting stoke was simple and solid. "I was always a good chipper and putter, simply because I was too lazy to practice the long game," he told writer Al Barkow in *Golf's Greatest Eighteen*. "I just hung around the green chipping and putting."

When Casper won his first U.S. Open, at Winged Foot in 1959—by one shot from Bob Rosburg and two from Mike Souchak and Claude Harmon—he had only 114 putts for four rounds, an average of 28.5 putts per round.

But no more was Casper's sharp, short game and steely nerves on show than during his second U.S. Open triumph, in 1966 at San Francisco's Olympic Club.

In fact, Casper won it from nowhere. Arnold Palmer led

by seven shots with nine holes to play. Legend has it he started thinking about Ben Hogan's record U.S. Open–winning score of 276. Casper says he saw Palmer begin to panic as he whittled away his lead: "Once it looked like I might get into his lead, his swing got shorter and faster and even with a two-iron he was pull-hooking into the rough, which was very deep at Olympic that year."

On the sixteenth hole, Palmer pulled one into heavy rough and Casper picked up three shots. Palmer hooked his tee shot left again on both seventeen and eighteen, and, all of a sudden, the scores were tied after seventy-two holes. In fact, Palmer had to hole a testing five-foot putt to force a play-off. Palmer played the final nine holes in four-over-par 39, while Casper shot 32.

In the play-off the following day, Palmer led by two strokes with nine to play, but then shot 40 to Casper's 34. Casper was not intimidated by Palmer's reputation but went about his game in a methodical way, aided and abetted by a putting technique he knew he could rely on.

If Casper's image needed a lift, it came from, of all people, a doctor. For much of his professional career, Casper had struggled with headaches, exhaustion, and sinus problems, and a meeting with an allergist determined that he was sensitive to, among other things, grass, lamb, apples, sugar, eggs, fruits, and wheat. The doctor put Casper on a diet of wild game and organically grown foods. He became famous for his eclectic and alternative tastes—venison, buffalo, bear, moose, elk, even hippopotamus. All of a sudden, his nickname became "Buffalo Bill."

Casper once said, "When you come down to it, there are only four interests in my life: religion, family, golf, and fishing, in that order." He and his wife, Shirley, had eleven children, six of them adopted. Little things matter.

Killing Giants

...............●...............

I'm very lucky. If it wasn't for golf I don't know what I'd be doing. If my IQ had been two points lower, I'd have been a plant somewhere.

LEE TREVINO, *THEY CALL ME SUPER MEX*

Whip the gringo!

LEE TREVINO'S FANS, URGING HIM ON DURING THE 1968 U.S. OPEN AT OAK HILL, NEW YORK STATE

Lee Trevino achieved far more in golf than a man with his humble beginnings and unusual outside-in swing probably should have. In fact, Trevino did something that no one else was able to do: he beat the world's best player, Jack Nicklaus, repeatedly.

Trevino grew up dirt poor in Dallas, Texas. His house had no electricity and no running water. Trevino, who had a Mexican lineage, never knew his father and was raised by his mother, Juanita, and his grandfather, Joe, a gravedigger. "My family was so poor they couldn't afford kids," Trevino said once. "The lady next door had me."

Trevino worked in the Texas cotton fields as a youngster and left school at fourteen for a life as a caddie at the Dallas Athletic Club. Once the course had been vacated, he played holes with the greenkeeper's son. Trevino earned $30 a week as a caddie and a shoeshiner but topped off his regular pay by betting people that he could beat them on a par-three course using a taped-up bottle instead of a club, getting a shot a hole. He regularly played the course in two or three over par, so he generally won the bets.

From this modest start in life, Trevino went on to play on the PGA Tour for 22 years, during which he won 27 times. Among these victories were two each of the U.S. Open, the British Open, and the PGA. The Masters, he always contended, did not suit his low left-to-right game, and the lack of rough at

Augusta favored a long hitter, which—at 5'7" tall—he wasn't. He turned down several invitations to attend The Masters, something he later said he regretted.

At the 1975 Western Open, while waiting out a rain delay near the thirteenth green, Trevino and his playing partners, Jerry Heard and Bobby Nichols, were hit by lightning that had traveled across a lake and up through the steel clubs in their bags. Trevino remembers being lifted off the ground, his ears jangling, and not being able to breathe. The emergency room doctor later apologized that he had no experience with lightning victims, saying, "They normally go straight to the morgue."

"When God wants to play through, you let Him," said Trevino.

But for all his quips and incessant on-course chatter, Trevino has a record that passes every test of golfing greatness. Of his six wins in major tournaments, four came while playing head-to-head against Jack Nicklaus.

First up, Trevino beat Nicklaus by four shots in the 1968 U.S. Open at Oak Hill in upper New York State, shooting four rounds in the sixties—the first time this had been done in the championship. He realized that winning the U.S. Open had changed things for him, but he put a Trevinoesque slant on it: "I played the tour in 1967 and told jokes and nobody laughed. Then I won the Open the next year, told the same jokes, and everybody laughed like hell."

Then, in the play-off for the 1971 U.S. Open at Philadelphia's Merion, Trevino beat Nicklaus by three shots after both were tied at 280 after four rounds. This was the start of a remarkable run by Trevino, who, in one 24-day stretch, won the U.S. Open, the Canadian Open in Montreal, and the British Open at Royal Birkdale.

The following year, Trevino again prevailed over Nicklaus, this time by a single stroke at the British Open at Muirfield. The key hole was the seventeenth. Trevino's fourth shot lay on a fluffy bank behind the green, from where he chipped in for par. "I thought I'd blown it at the seventeenth green when I drove into a trap. God is a Mexican," Trevino said afterward. Notably, Nicklaus had already won The Masters and the U.S. Open when he arrived at Muirfield, so Trevino's win killed his chances for the Grand Slam.

Finally, Trevino triumphed over Nicklaus by a shot in the 1974 PGA at Tanglewood Country Club in North Carolina.

Trevino said there were no secrets to his success against Nicklaus: "There was nothing psychological about it. There was no gamesmanship. I kept it in the fairway. . . . I don't care if a guy hits it 40 yards longer; if he's in the woods, I'm going to win that hole. If you hit every fairway, eventually you're going to beat a guy."

Smashing Barriers

············●············

Sifford was a very talented player whose trademark cigar seemed to be eternally short, perhaps because he got so many doors slammed in his face.

DAN GLEASON, *THE GREAT, THE GRAND AND THE ALSO-RAN*, 1976

The first time I played there, back in 1959, I'll never forget it. People looked at me as if I had a tail.

CHARLIE SIFFORD, ON BEING AN EARLY BLACK GOLFER AT THE U.S. OPEN AT WINGED FOOT

Charlie Sifford spent most of his life as a black man in a white man's world. Born in Charlotte, North Carolina, in 1922, Sifford began caddying at the age of thirteen. Like many other promising young black golfers, he entered tournaments that black golfers organized among themselves. The reality was that there was nowhere else to go; they were officially excluded from the PGA Tour. Article 2, Section III of the PGA Constitution specified: "For professionals of the Caucasian race."

Occasionally, Sifford was allowed to enter a "normal" professional tournament, but he was invariably heckled and jostled. Sometimes he received death threats.

That he was a good player was beyond doubt. He won the United Golf Association (UGA) National Negro Open six times in the 1950s—five times in a row from 1952 to 1956. And in 1957, he won the Long Beach Open, which was cosponsored by the PGA but was not an official PGA Tour event.

Sifford recalls the challenges of playing in one of these "normal" tournaments, the 1959 Greater Greensboro Open:

> I was going good. Suddenly I was intercepted by
> five white men who started following me around

171

the course. They threw their beer cans at me and called me nigger and other names. This went on for several holes and they were finally arrested, but, after I lost a lot of strokes and finished far down the list.

In 1961, California's attorney general applied pressure on the PGA to alter its constitution to allow black golfers full membership on the tour. Sifford became a fully fledged member and went on to win two official money events—the 1967 Greater Hartford Open and the 1969 Los Angeles Open. Watching Sifford and other black golfers closely were the members of Augusta National, which runs The Masters. The *Chicago Tribune* quoted Augusta's founder, Clifford Roberts, as saying: "As long as I live we'll have nothing but black caddies and white players."

In 1971, however, The Masters amended its rules to state that anyone who won a major PGA Tour event would automatically qualify for an invitation. But the rule wasn't retrospective. Neither Sifford's previous victories nor those of another great black player, Pete Brown, counted. Sifford would never play in The Masters.

It became apparent that the man most likely to break through for a win was Lee Elder, a black golfer from Dallas. But it was not going to be easy. In 1973, Elder tied for second in the USI Classic in Sutton, Massachusetts. Then he lost a sudden-death play-off in the Greater Hartford Open to Lee Trevino. He finished fourth at the Colonial and fifth at the Crosby.

Then, in April 1974, Elder played in the Monsanto Open at Pensacola, Florida, a course that, only a few years earlier, had barred black players from its clubhouse. It looked like Elder's run of near misses would continue when England's Peter Oosterhuis had a one-and-a-half foot putt on the final hole to win the tournament, but he missed. Oosterhuis missed two more short putts during the sudden-death play-off. On the fourth play-off hole, Elder sank a twenty-foot putt to win, and the crowd went wild. Elder cried.

The following year, on April 10, Elder teed off at The Masters, the first black golfer to do so. He shot 74 and 78 to miss the cut by four, but that didn't matter. What mattered was that he was playing, and that he paved the way for other black golfers like Jim Thorpe and Calvin Peete.

That same year, 1975, a baby was born to a Thai mother and a black father in Cypress, California—they called him Tiger

Woods. When Woods won his first Masters in 1997—shooting eighteen-under par for a twelve-shot victory, the biggest in a major in 127 years—he said: "I was the first one to ever win, but I wasn't the pioneer. Charlie Sifford, Lee Elder, Ted Rhodes, those are the guys who paved the way for me. Because of what Elder did, I was able to play here."

Sifford said of Woods's win: "As far as I'm concerned, it put The Masters to rest for me. I've been waiting 35 years."

In 2004, Sifford became the first black inductee to the World Golf Hall of Fame in St Augustine, Florida. Elder said, "It just goes to show you how long it takes sometimes to accomplish certain things."

Handling
Disappointment

············●············

Over the years, I've studied habits of golfers. I know what to look for.

Watch their eyes. Fear shows up

when there is an enlargement of the pupils.

Big pupils lead to big scores.

SAM SNEAD

Class is the ability to handle pressure with grace.

So what did I do? I just did what comes naturally.

I vomited.

CHARLES PRICE AFTER THE 1963 BRITISH OPEN

No one who saw them will ever forget the events that unfolded in 15 minutes of madness on Sunday, July 18, 1999, during the closing stages of the British Open at Carnoustie in Scotland. The mere mention of it sends a chill down the most hardened golfing spine.

Frenchman Jean van de Velde stood on the tee of the par-four eighteenth hole with a three-shot lead. Surely the tournament was all over. A drive, a layup in front of the green, a simple pitch and two putts, and history would show that the first Frenchman to win the British Open since Arnaud Massey at Royal Liverpool in 1907 had done it easy.

Van de Velde's first three rounds of 75, 68, and 70 had put him at level par, leading the tournament by five shots. During the final round, he had given up two of those shots but now required nothing worse than a double bogey to win—and he had birdied the eighteenth twice during the previous three rounds.

Television commentators were impressed with the way in which van de Velde had carried himself during the tournament, on a course that is acknowledged as the toughest on the British Open rotation. "We have an underdog with a steely look about him," said veteran commentator Peter Alliss as van de Velde strode to the final hole after recording fighting pars on the fifteenth, sixteenth, and seventeenth—arguably the sternest finish in golf. "He's a pretty cool customer right now."

But Alliss added this rider: "One of the dangers for van de Velde now is not to get carried away by the adulation of the multitude before the job is done." What happened next was the most excruciating quarter of an hour in golf history.

To the surprise of many, van de Velde hit a driver off the final tee. He blocked it right, but his ball avoided the Barry Burn, which wends its way around the last hole. He then sliced his second shot, a two-iron, and watched in horror as his ball bounced backward off a spectator stand into heavy rough. He then slashed his ball into the burn in front of the green and, as thousands of spectators watched slack-jawed, took off his socks and shoes to play his half-submerged ball. Australian Craig Parry, van de Velde's playing partner, suggested that he wait a few hours for the tide to recede.

Sanity prevailed, and van de Velde took a penalty drop back in the rough, then hacked his ball into a greenside bunker. He exploded out and holed a difficult putt for a seven. The score got him into a four-hole play-off against Scotsman Paul Lawrie, who had started the day ten shots behind the

Frenchman, and American Justin Leonard. Lawrie won the play-off by three shots.

The media commentary from the championship's finale was brutal. "There have been momentous mess-ups on the final hole, but this would rank with the best of them. You get your money's worth from the French," said one commentator. Curtis Strange, a golf analyst for ABC-TV and two-time U.S. Open champion, called van de Velde's decision to use a driver off the final tee as "the biggest sports debacle of all time."

Van de Velde took all this in stride:

> It is a golf tournament. It's a game. And I gave it my best shot. There are worse things in life. [Carnoustie] was a great test, a very difficult test. We knew sooner or later we were going to run into a wall. Unfortunately, it happened on the 72nd. Maybe it was asking too much for me. Maybe I should have laid up. The ball was lying so well . . . Next time, I hit a wedge, and you all forgive me?
>
> There are a lot of people who wrote that I should feel very proud of what I did, my attitude was exceptional, and people should learn from it.

One guy wrote me a few weeks later, and he said,
"Thanks for reminding me it's a game, because
since then, I'm playing even better and enjoying
it more."

The comment that really ate at van de Velde was this:
"He could have played the entire hole with his putter and
gotten under seven." Five months later, in the dead of winter,
the Frenchman returned to Carnoustie to test the hypothesis.
"Perhaps give me a pencil and a scorecard and then I can put
my score down and probably send it to the R&A and see what
they can do for Christmas for me," he said to the Carnoustie
starter before going out to play his one hole with his one club.
"If I drive in the burn, come and rescue me, OK?"

On his third attempt, he succeeded.

Dealing with Criticism

...............●...............

Pick up the ball, have the clubs destroyed, and leave the course.

VISCOUNT CASTLEROSSE TO HIS CADDIE AFTER
HITTING A BALL INTO THE HEATHER ON WALTON
HEATH IN THE 1930s

Golf is an open exhibition of overweening ambition, courage deflated by stupidity, skill soured by a whiff of arrogance. These humiliations are the essence of the game.

ALISTAIR COOKE

On the East Coast of the United States, within the gently rolling landscape off Peconic Bay on Long Island, about 100 miles from New York City, lies the National Golf Links of America, known simply as The National. The course is intensely private and prestigious and is spoken of in the same breath as Augusta National in Georgia, Pine Valley in Philadelphia, and Shinnecock Hills, The National's Long Island neighbor.

The course, with its imposing, presumptuous name, was the brainchild of Charles Blair Macdonald, who was born in Ontario in 1855 and grew up in Chicago. In 1872, aged sixteen, he was sent to St. Andrews University in Scotland and took up golf with a fanatical intensity; he was tutored by Old Tom Morris, no less. In 1892, Macdonald founded the Chicago Golf Club, and in 1895 he won the first U.S. Amateur Championship at the Newport Country Club on Rhode Island, beating Charles Sands, 12 and 11—still the tournament's record-winning margin.

Macdonald eventually decided to build a course on Long Island, and he traveled to Britain over five summers to study the greatest links and the best holes. He also enlisted the help of seventy wealthy sportsmen—including W.K. Vanderbilt (who made his fortune in railroads), Clarence Mackay (mining and telegraph), Charles Deering (farm machinery), and Harry

Payne Whitney (streetcars and thoroughbred racing)—each of whom contributed $1,000 to the cause.

Construction of The National began in 1907, and play began two years later, with members arriving by private yacht. Today, the front porch of the imposing National clubhouse still holds the telescope originally installed there. Modern-day visitors see another strange piece of history as soon as they enter the front gates—an enormous red-and-gray-shingled windmill situated between the second fairway and the sixteenth green.

History has it that, while playing the second hole not long after the club opened, a member by the name of Dan Pomeroy, the president of publishing company Condé Nast, hooked his ball left and hit a water barrel in the rough. Pomeroy suggested to Macdonald that the barrel should be covered by something and thought that a windmill would be an appropriate structure. Later, when Macdonald was in Europe, he took Pomeroy's advice. He bought a windmill and had it shipped to Long Island and erected on the course.

When opening his next bill from the club, Pomeroy was a little startled to see that it included the cost of the windmill—$10,000. Needless to say, he paid up.

Laughter

............●.............

Golf's a hard game to figure. One day you slice it, shank it, hit into all the traps and miss every green. And the next day, you go out and for no reason at all, you really stink.

BOB HOPE

It's wonderful how you can start out with three strangers in the morning, play eighteen holes, and by the time the day is over, you have three solid enemies.

BOB HOPE

Legendary comedian and entertainer Bob Hope was a fine golfer in his prime, competing in the 1951 British Amateur as well as many other top-class amateur tournaments. He died in 2003, aged 100. His jokes fill 85,000 pages in the archives of the Library of Congress.

Apart from humor, Hope's major passion was golf. He could, of course, combine the two and did so for many years. "If you watch a game, it's fun. If you play it, it's recreation. If you work at it, it's golf," he was fond of saying. In his advancing years, he said, "I've been playing the game so long that my handicap is in Roman numerals," and, "I'd give up golf if I didn't have so many sweaters."

In 1960, Hope began hosting a tournament on the PGA Tour, the Bob Hope Classic, which still exists today. It is a pro-am event, which meant it was tailor-made for Hope's brand of humor. There's nothing like a bunch of amateurs playing golf if you're looking to poke fun at someone.

Even presidents were fair game. "I played with [President Eisenhower] yesterday. It's hard to beat a guy who rattles his medals while you're putting," Hope said once.

As for Vice President Spiro Agnew, Hope said, "When Agnew yelled 'Fore!' you never knew whether he was telling someone to get out of the way or if he was predicting how many spectators he would hit with the shot." Hope said Agnew "had a black belt" in golf, sometimes "playing three or four courses at one time, as well as the practice fairway."

But Hope reserved his best presidential lines for Gerald Ford, who played in Hope's tournament in 1977, not long after he left office. One of Ford's errant shots hit some spectators, causing Hope to describe Ford as "the man who made golf a contact sport."

Ford's golf opened up a whole new line of gags for Hope, including: "Whenever I play with him, I usually try to make it a foursome—the President, myself, a paramedic, and a faith healer"; "It's not hard to find Gerald Ford on a golf course. Just follow the wounded"; and "You don't know what fear is until you hear Ford behind you shouting, 'Fore!' and you're still in the locker room."

Versatility

...........•...........

Golfers belong to an exclusive universal club. . . .
Their connection is not bound by time or geography.
It is the spirit and the joy of the game.

J.P. RESNICK, EDITOR OF *THE LITTLE TREASURY OF GOLF*

The greatest thing about owning your own course
is that par can be whatever you want it to be.
This hole here, for example, is a par 47.
And yesterday I birdied the sucker.

SINGER WILLIE NELSON

It was no surprise that when Captain Alan Shepard, the commander of *Apollo 14*, decided to do something unusual on the moon in 1971, he chose to play golf. With a club (a one-iron attached to a makeshift shaft) held in one hand, he whacked a ball about 220 yards with his first shot. His only other shot was a shank.

When he returned to Earth, the Royal and Ancient Golf Club of St. Andrews sent him a telegram: "Please refer to *Rules of Golf* section on etiquette, paragraph six, quote, before leaving a bunker, a player should carefully fill up all holes made by him therein, unquote."

The beauty of golf is that, as Shepard demonstrated, it can be played anywhere, for any reason.

Just ask the indefatigable Floyd Rood. In 1964, he took 479 days to golf his way 3,399 miles across the United States. His score: 114,737. Penalty shots: 3,511. Injuries: two sore arms and bunions.

Ten years later, two Californian teenagers, Bob Aube and Phil Marrone, golfed their way from San Francisco to Los Angeles, playing the 497-yard "hole" in 16 days, the first six along freeways. Their scores are unrecorded, but they used more than 1,000 balls.

People have hit balls from the tops of the Pyramids, across the gorge at Victoria Falls, and from atop city buildings. Before the 1977 Lancôme Trophy in Paris, Arnold Palmer hit three balls from the second story of the Eiffel Tower, more than 330 feet above the ground. The longest hit traveled 383 yards. He hooked one ball, which hit a bus, but the traffic had been stopped for safety reasons, and there were no injuries.

In the mid-1960s, a member of the New York Rangers hockey team hit a ball from the top of 10,990-foot Mount Edith Cavell in Alberta, Canada. The ball struck the Ghost Glacier, nearly 5,000 feet below, then bounced off a rocky ledge and disappeared.

The game is also tailor-made for other challenges. In 1971, during one 24-hour period, Australian marathon runner Ian Colston played 401 holes using only a six-iron over the Bendigo course in Victoria. And in 1991, Brits Simon Gard, Nick Harley, and brothers Patrick and Alistair Maxwell completed 14 rounds in one day at Iceland's Akureyri Golf Club, the most northerly course in the world.

Of course, playing several rounds on the same day doesn't require them to be played on the same course, or even in the same country. In 1974, Irishmen E.S. Wilson and

G.W. Donaldson played seven nine-hole matches on different courses in seven parts of the United Kingdom—La Moye in the Channel Islands (a British dependency), Hawarden (Wales), Chester (England), Turnberry (Scotland), Castletown (Isle of Man, another British dependency), Dundalk (Ireland), and Warrenpoint (Northern Ireland). They teed off at first light and finished at 9:25 p.m. Wilson piloted his own aeroplane throughout.

And you can play quickly if you like. The fastest round ever recorded was by Dick Kimbrough, who in 1972 played the 6,371-yard course at North Platte Country Club in Nebraska in thirty minutes and ten seconds, using only a three-iron.

And what about playing in unusual clothes? In 1912, Harry Dearth wore a complete suit of heavy armor while playing a match at Bushey Hall in Hertfordshire, North London. He lost, 2 and 1.

Cross-country challenges are another option. In 1920, Rupert Phillips and Raymond Thomas teed up at the first hole of Radyr Golf Club in Wales and played to the last hole at Southerndown, a straight-line distance of fifteen-and-a-half miles. Along the way, they negotiated swamps, woods, and plowed fields. They had a wager that they would not do the "hole" in fewer than 1,000 strokes. They took fewer than 700.

189

In 1953, the Golden Ball competition was held in Ireland, which involved players hitting off the first tee at Kildare Golf Club and playing over hill and down dale before holing out on the eighteenth hole at the Curragh Club, five miles away. The organizers advertised a million pounds for anyone who could get a hole in one. The event was won by Irish international Joe Carr. His score: 52.

Making a Habit
of Success

............●............

My game had gotten so good and so dependable that there were

times when I actually would get bored playing. I'd hit it in the

fairway, on the green, make birdie or par, and go to the next hole.

BYRON NELSON, *HOW I PLAYED THE GAME*

As a competitor, Byron was able to be mean and

tough and intimidating and pleasant.

KEN VENTURI

Byron Nelson didn't have a long career—it lasted only eleven

seasons—but no one will ever beat the year he had in 1945. He won eighteen tournaments, eleven of them in a row. The best streak of wins since then is six, by Tiger Woods in 2000. Nelson won five of those tournaments by seven or more strokes. During his winning streak, he played nine stroke-play events in 109 under par.

During 1945, Nelson—a tall, slim man from Fort Worth, Texas, who had not been allowed to fight in World War II because of a blood condition—also set records for the lowest tournament score (259, twenty-one under par in Seattle) and the lowest single-season stroke average (68.34), which stood until Woods broke it. He had 100 subpar rounds out of 112 rounds played, including a 62. Over the course of the year, he finished second seven times. But in actual fact, Nelson's amazing play started in 1944 and continued well into 1946.

In 1944, 22 events were played. Nelson won eight of them. Overall, he was either first, second, or third in 17 tournaments. His worst finish that year was a tie for sixth.

In 1945, Nelson's five-month streak began on March 11, when he won the Miami Four-Ball with Jug McSpaden. He then beat Sam Snead in a play-off, over 36 holes, at the Charlotte Open. His roll continued as he won the Greensboro Open by eight strokes, the Durham Open by five, the Atlanta Open by nine, the Montreal Open by 10, the Philadelphia Invitational by two, the Chicago Victory Open by seven, the Tam O'Shanter in Chicago by 11, and the Canadian Open by four.

In between, he won the PGA in Dayton, Ohio, which was then a match-play event, cleaning up, in this order, Gene Sarazen, Mike Turnesa, Denny Shute, Claude Harmon, and Sam Byrd. It wasn't until August 19 that Nelson returned to Earth, tying for fourth at Memphis. Incidentally, the following week, he won the Knoxville Invitational by 10 strokes, competing against a field that included Snead and Ben Hogan.

The last two events Nelson entered in 1945—the Seattle Open and the Glen Garden Invitational in Fort Worth—he won by 13 shots and eight shots, respectively. He then won the first two events of 1946, the Los Angeles Open at Riviera by five shots and the San Francisco Open at Olympic by nine shots, giving him another nice little streak of four wins.

In February 1946, he tied for thirteenth at Pensacola— the only time he finished out of the top ten in three years—prompting Jimmy Demaret to say, "I've been telling you all along he's overrated." Nelson ended up entering 21 tournaments in 1946, and he won six of them. He retired at the end of that year, aged only thirty-four.

Of the 72 tournaments Nelson entered between 1944 and 1946, he won 32 of them. He was either first, second, or third 57 times.

In 2005, on the 60th anniversary of his record year, Nelson was asked if he ever thought that, at age ninety-three, he would look back on the 1945 season to find that no one had matched it. Nelson smiled and replied, to much laughter, "I never thought about the fact I'd live to be ninety-three."

Endurance

...............●...............

No matter what happens, keep on hitting the ball.

HARRY VARDON

No virtue in the world is so oft rewarded as perseverance.

BOBBY JONES

On a sunny morning in 1951, a group of golfers, photographers, and curious onlookers gathered on the brick balcony of the Royal and Ancient Golf Club in St. Andrews to watch a portly man in a flat cap, glasses, and thick tweed trousers tee off. The golfer's swing was compact and neat, and his drive flew long and straight, slightly left of center, toward the Old Course's famous Swilken Bridge.

The man was Ralph Kennedy, a founding member of Winged Foot Golf Club in New York, and the reason for the crowd was that Kennedy was playing his 3000th course, a task that had taken him 43 years.

In 1910, aged twenty-eight, Kennedy played his first course, Van Cortlandt Park, in the New York City borough of the Bronx. His score was 146, and like many beginners, he was hooked. By the time he had ended his quest to play as many golf courses as possible, aged seventy-two, he had tackled 3,165 of them. The last course he played was Hamilton Inn in New York State.

Kennedy played his 1,000th course in 1932, on his fiftieth birthday, and his 2,000th course eight years later. He took another six years to get to the 2,500 mark, and then a further five years to get to 3,000. Kennedy played in 14 countries, with most of his rounds recorded in the United States, Mexico, Canada, Central America, South America, Bermuda, and Britain.

One day in Illinois, he played five courses. Another day in Arkansas, he played four rounds. He played eight courses in

Bermuda over two days, 21 courses in Chicago in a week, and 31 courses over nine days in Maine.

Not one for half measures, Kennedy dated and signed the scorecards for each round, which he kept in a safe. He eventually donated them to the USGA museum in Far Hills, New Jersey. They remain one of the museum's more unusual collections, and probably the most hard-earned.

Silencing the Doubters

···········•···········

I never thought his short game was very good.
Of course, he hit so many damn greens, it didn't make any
difference.

TOM WATSON ON JACK NICKLAUS, *GOLF DIGEST*, 1983

To win the things he's won, build golf courses around the world,
be a daddy to all those kids, and be a hell of an investor, too. It's
phenomenal. Hey, stick a broom in his rear end and he could
probably sweep the USA.

JACKIE BURKE ON JACK NICKLAUS, *GOLF MAGAZINE*, 1981

One morning before the 1986 Masters at Augusta, Georgia, 46-year-old Jack Nicklaus noticed a newspaper clipping on the fridge door of his family's rented house. The story from the *Atlanta Constitution*, which had been stuck on the fridge by a friend, said, among other things, that Nicklaus was "done, through, washed up and finished." The implication was clear—that the 17-time major winner had no business taking a spot from some young tyro in the coveted Masters field.

As Nicklaus later recalled, "It made me stew for a while, but in the end I thought that maybe the writer Tom McAllister has a point." He had then set about proving McAllister wrong.

History was against Nicklaus. He had won five previous Masters tournaments, but his most recent victory had been in 1975—eleven years earlier—when he was fitter and stronger. It had been six years since he had won a major. Equally tellingly, it had been two years since Nicklaus had won an event on the US tour—the Memorial Tournament in 1984. In 1985, he had only managed a 44th placing on the money list, his best results having been a tie for second in the Canadian Open and another second in the Greater Milwaukee Open.

The first few months of 1986 didn't point to a change of fortune. After missed cuts at Pebble Beach, the Honda, and the Tournament Players Championship, he withdrew at New Orleans because of his mother-in-law's death. He tied for 39th at Hawaii and came 47th at Doral and 16th at Phoenix. Here, surely, was a golfer marking time before joining the Senior PGA Tour.

Nicklaus's first three rounds at the 1986 Masters—74, 71, and 69—while solid, did not suggest anything extraordinary. With a round to go, he lay in ninth position, four shots behind leader Greg Norman. Ahead of him were other golfing luminaries such as Nick Price—who shot a 63 in the third round—Bernhard Langer, Seve Ballesteros, Tom Kite, and Tom Watson.

Nicklaus's first nine holes of the final round on April 13 again produced nothing spectacular, with eight straight pars and a birdie on nine. But the old saying that The Masters doesn't start until the back nine on the final day was never truer than on that day. In two urgent hours, Nicklaus shot birdie, birdie, bogey, birdie, par, eagle, birdie, birdie, par. A back nine of 30 gave him a 65 and a one-shot victory over Tom Kite and Greg Norman. The roars could be heard in downtown Augusta. It was the lowest final round for a win at The Masters since Gary Player shot 64 in 1978.

Nicklaus became the oldest winner of the tournament. Tom McAllister of the *Atlanta Constitution* ate humble pie for weeks.

Surrendering One's Youth

...............●...............

My handicap? Arthritis.

BOBBY JONES, AGED FORTY-FIVE

The older you get, the longer you used to be.

CHI CHI RODRIGUEZ, *PGA TOUR NEWS*

Irishman Joe Carr won his first significant tournament, the East of Ireland Amateur, in 1941 at the age of nineteen. He went on to win a total of twelve East of Ireland titles, twelve West of Ireland titles, six Irish Amateur Close Championships, four Irish Amateur Opens, and three South of Ireland titles.

Carr also won the British Amateur three times (in 1953, 1958, and 1960), made the semifinal at the 1961 U.S. Amateur, and was low amateur in both the 1956 and 1958 British Opens. He played in the Walker Cup ten times. In 1961, he was the first non-American to receive the Bobby Jones Award for distinguished sportsmanship in golf, the United States Golf Association's highest honor.

Twenty-five years after his last East of Ireland victory, when his game was losing its sharpness, Carr was playing a social game at County Louth Golf Club. Midround, his young caddie asked: "Have you ever played here before?"

"Yes," said Carr, "as a matter of fact I have."

"Did you ever play in the East of Ireland Championship?" asked the boy.

"Yes I did," replied Carr, a little testily.

"Did you ever do any good?" the caddie asked.

"I won it twelve times," said Carr with some satisfaction, hoping that might end the conversation.

There was a moment's silence before the boy piped up again: "Well, the standard must have been much worse in your day."

Longevity

...........•...........

Talk to the ball. "This isn't going to hurt a bit," I tell the ball under my breath. "Sambo is just going to give you a nice little ride."

SAM SNEAD, *THE EDUCATION OF A GOLFER*

Sam is the one new player since 1930 with that evanescent but definite quality, magnetism, which lures fans from miles around to the tournaments and sustains them every shot of the way.

GENE SARAZEN, *THIRTY YEARS OF CHAMPIONSHIP GOLF*

It was a delicious quirk of fate that three of the world's best golfers—Sam Snead, Ben Hogan, and Byron Nelson—were born within six months of each other in 1912. Among them, they would dominate golf for a generation, collectively winning more than 300 tournaments, including 21 major championships.

But despite their similar beginnings and comparable successes, they ended their careers very differently. For while Nelson packed in the game in 1946 and Hogan's career was effectively over by the late 1950s, Snead kept playing until the late 1970s.

For golfing longevity, it's hard to hold a candle to Samuel Jackson Snead. He won tournaments in six different decades—135 victories worldwide in all. He led the money-winning list three times, took the Vardon Trophy (for the lowest stroke average) four times, played on the American Ryder Cup team eight times in a period spanning 18 years, and won the World Seniors five times. And he played against great golfers in several eras, from Walter Hagen and Gene Sarazen in his early days, to Tom Watson and Seve Ballesteros in his twilight years.

Snead's ability to stay in the game long after his peers had given it away was mostly the result of a flexibility and an agility that others didn't possess. Famously, he could kick a door lintel six-and-a-half feet high, and he could pick a golf ball out of a hole without bending his knees.

He also had a relaxed, homespun approach to life, which reflected his lazy but powerful swing. Watching Snead's self-taught swing was to witness a slow gathering of power and a rhythmic release. "Take it easily and lazily, because the golf ball isn't going to run away from you while you're swinging," he wrote in his 1946 book, *How to Play Golf*. Writer Bernard Darwin said watching Snead's swing brought "tears of joy to the eyes."

Snead, born in 1912, grew up near the Back Creek Mountains of Virginia in the days of the Great Depression. "Where I lived, near Bald Knob, the roads got littler and littler until they just ran up a tree," he wrote in his book *The Education of a Golfer*.

He shot raccoons and bears for the dinner table, ate squirrel soup, and tried to keep clear of the moonshiners and their illicit stills in the hills. At the age of seven, he began caddying at The Homestead in Hot Springs. He fashioned his first golf club from the limb of a swamp maple, leaving the bark on for a grip. Through trial and error, he developed a roundhouse baseball-type swing, and using hand-me-down clubs, he hit the ball startling distances. "Ah jes' takes that club back nice and lazy and then ah try to whop it down on the barrelhead," he once said.

Snead won a job as an assistant professional at the nearby Greenbrier Hotel in White Sulphur Springs, West Virginia, and then nearly lost it in his first week. Playing the 328-yard par-four fifth hole, Snead drove the green. His ball landed near Alva Bradley, president of the Cleveland Indians baseball club and director of the Chesapeake & Ohio Railroad, the company that owned the Greenbrier Hotel. Bradley dressed Snead down for hitting up on him. Snead's answer—"I didn't expect my drive to go so far"—brought sniggers from the group, and he was asked to do it again. He did, and a remarkable career was launched.

In 1936, Snead won the West Virginia Closed Championship, which included a round of 61—then thought to be a world record. The following year, aged twenty-four, he ventured out west to try the tour with $300 of Greenbrier member money in his pocket. He didn't expect to last long but then made $600 in his first week. Three weeks later he collected $1,200 for winning the Oakland Open, beating Johnny Revolta and Ralph Guldahl.

Afterward, Henry Picard showed Snead a picture of himself in the *New York Times*. Snead's folksy response—"How did they get that? I ain't never been to New York"—endeared him to golf fans everywhere. His straw hat became as much a signature as his power hitting. Once he played a round at Augusta in bare feet and shot 68.

Snead was aware of his reputation for power hitting—he had been given the nickname Slammin' Sam—and felt obliged to live up to it. It didn't help that tournament organizers paired him with long hitters like Jimmy Thomson and Lawson Little. His form slumped. Picard thought that the shaft of his driver was too whippy and sold him a heavier and stiff-shafted Izett driver for $5.50. Snead stayed faithful to the club for years, regularly gluing up the head when cracks appeared. "That act of generosity by the Hershey Hurricane could never be repaid, because that No. 1 wood was the single greatest discovery I ever made in golf and put me on the road to happy times," he wrote.

Although he won many tournaments, he found it hard to achieve a breakthrough in a major. In 1938, he lost in the final of the PGA to Paul Runyan. The next year, he came in second in The Masters to Ralph Guldahl by a stroke, and in 1940 he was runner-up again in the PGA, this time to Byron Nelson. The press labelled him a "choker." However, in 1942, he beat Jim Turnesa in the final of the PGA, and his career took off.

Despite his career victories—which included three Masters, three PGAs, and the 1946 British Open at St. Andrews—Snead never won a U.S. Open. During 26 attempts, he came in second four times, including when he lost an 18-hole play-off in 1947 to Lew Worsham and in 1949 at Medinah Country Club, when he missed a three-foot putt on the final hole to lose to Cary Middlecoff.

In 1953 at Oakmont, he was a stroke behind with a round to go but shot 76 and lost by six strokes to Ben Hogan. When asked afterward if he had been tight before the round, he replied famously, "Tight? I was so tight you couldn't a drove a flaxseed up my ass with a knot maul."

But no U.S. Open loss hurt him more than the one in 1939, when he needed a par five on the last hole at Spring Mill, Philadelphia. Thinking a birdie was required, he went for distance off the tee, drove into the rough, hacked into a bunker, left it in, and eventually three-putted for an eight, handing the title to Byron Nelson.

"It's the Opens I let slip away that hurt the most. Not a day goes by when I don't think about that, I reckon," he told writer James Dodson.

While his contemporaries decided to retire from the game, Snead kept playing and kept winning, despite a well-publicized battle with the putting yips. He became the oldest player to win a PGA Tour event when he won the 1965 Greater Greensboro Open at the age of fifty-two years and ten months.

Aged sixty-two, he shot a one-under-par 279 to tie for third in the PGA at Tanglewood, North Carolina, three shots behind Lee Trevino. Five years later, aged sixty-seven, he became the oldest player to make the cut at a major championship—the 1979 PGA at Oakland Hills, which was eventually won by David Graham.

Later that year, 54 years after his first victory, he shot his age—67—in the Quad Cities Open, a regular tournament on the US tour; the next day, he shot 66. Four years later, at age seventy-one, he shot a round of 60, and when he was eighty-four, he shot a 66. "The road's getting shorter and narrower, but I'll play wherever the pigeons land," he said in his advancing years.

Snead died in 2002, aged eighty-nine.

Defying Your Age

............●............

Golf is the only game in the world where a man of sixty can play with
the best. That's why golf is such a great game. And no one has ever
licked it.

SAM SNEAD, *GOLF DIGEST*, 1975

I don't want to be eulogized until I'm dead.

BEN HOGAN, DECLINING AN INVITATION TO BE HONOREE
AT JACK NICKLAUS'S MEMORIAL TOURNAMENT

In 2007, something extraordinary happened on the Old Course
of Sunningdale Golf and Country Club in London, Ontario.

Ninety-three-year-old Ed Ervasti shot 72. In doing so, he broke his age by 21 strokes. You might need time to digest that.

Ervasti said of his round:

> I was three under par for the front nine including an eagle two on the second hole. I got a bit nervous on the back nine and I reached the last hole, a par five, needing a five to shoot par 72. I hit a terrible shot for my third and ended up in some long grass next to the green. I hit my fourth shot to two feet and got the putt.

Breaking your age is something that tends not to enter a person's thinking until they are in their seventies. That said, most people's games have deteriorated to a point where it's an academic exercise anyway. Estimates are that a person breaking their age happens once every 100,000 rounds of golf.

Ed Ervasti broke his age for more than two decades. When he was seventy-five, he won a tournament at his home club, the London Hunt and Country Club in southwest Ontario, shooting 75, 72, and 63. You might need time to digest that, as well.

Ervasti played off scratch for the best part of thirty years. In 1949, he won the Michigan Amateur, and he played in two U.S. Opens—the 1949 event at Medinah in Chicago, and in 1956 at Oak Hill in Rochester, New York. Between 1971 and 1980, he won six Canadian Seniors Golf Association championships. Later, he won four American Seniors Match Play Championships.

"Seniors golf is very popular in North America," he said. "Every week a club in Ontario has a senior tournament, so there were plenty of opportunities to play."

Ervasti played with many great players, including Byron Nelson, Arnold Palmer, Julius Boros, Ben Hogan, Bobby Locke, Ed Furgol, and Harvie Ward. He met Bobby Jones in 1942. He said the key to his golfing longevity was his short game:

> I'm only five foot eight inches and was never a big hitter, but I have always been a good chipper and putter. I used to practice my chipping for hours on end, and I holed a lot of bunker shots. I was still improving in my 50s and was still shooting par in my 70s and 80s. Playing good golf for a long

time is all about being patient. Golf is the most frustrating game there is. Temperament is crucial.

Ervasti conceded that his game deteriorated a little in his nineties—his scores were regularly in the mideighties. In 2009, he said:

> I had an artificial hip put in five years ago, which means my right knee can't kick in during my swing. When your legs lose their mobility, it's hard to play golf. You can't synchronize your body. I have certainly lost some distance from the tee. Moving from age 93 to 96 is a big step.

Ervasti died in May 2015, aged 101.

Knowing When to Quit

·············•·············

As a young man he was able to stand up to just about the best that life can offer, which is not easy, and later he stood up, with equal grace, to just about the worst.

HERBERT WARREN WIND ON BOBBY JONES

I wasn't quite certain what had happened or what I had done. I only knew that I had completed a period of most strenuous effort and that at this point, nothing more remained to be done.

BOBBY JONES AT MERION GOLF CLUB,

HAVING COMPLETED THE GRAND SLAM

On November 17, 1930, Herbert Ramsay, vice president of the USGA, made an announcement on behalf of the world's greatest golfer, 28-year-old Bobby Jones. The demands of Jones's law practice, Ramsay announced, had forced him to retire from competitive golf. So ended the career of an amateur golfer whose record, doubtless, will stand forever.

Other golfers have won more tournaments than Jones, including more majors, but no other golfer has ever won, in the same year, the British Amateur, the British Open, the U.S. Amateur and the U.S. Open. Writers borrowed a bridge term to describe Jones's annus mirabilis: the Grand Slam. George Trevor of the *New York Sun* preferred the "impregnable quadrilateral."

Jones's assault on the record began at the British Amateur in late May, 1930, on the Old Course at St. Andrews. His win, which left the town abuzz, required seven matches over five days, then a 36-hole final.

In the first round, Jones accounted for 30-year-old former miner Sidney Roper. Roper started with four pars and a birdie and found himself 3 down. Jones won the match on the sixteenth hole.

Jones waltzed through the second and third rounds but

in the fourth came up against Cyril Tolley, the reigning British Amateur champion. On the eighteenth green, Tolley had a 13-foot putt to win the match . . . and missed it. Jones won the match with the aid of a stymie on the next hole. Had Tolley's putt on the eighteenth hole dropped, the history of the game of golf would have been very different.

Jones was in trouble only once more during the tournament, when he found himself 2 down with five holes to play in the semifinal against George Voigt. He eventually won the match on the eighteenth. The final was something of an anticlimax, with Jones triumphing over Englishman Roger Wethered, 7 and 6. In so doing, Jones became only the third American to win the British Amateur title, after Walter Travis and Jess Sweetser.

Three weeks later, on Wednesday, June 18, Jones teed off at Royal Liverpool in the British Open. The eyes of the golfing world were on Jones—virtually anyone who had ever achieved anything in British golf traveled to Liverpool, including John Ball, Harold Hilton, Harry Vardon, James Braid, and Ted Ray.

He scored 70, 72, 74, and 75 to win by two strokes over Leo Diegel and Macdonald Smith. But it was not an easy win. Jones almost came undone in the final round with a seven at the eighth hole, taking five shots from the edge of the green. Writer Bernard Darwin observed, "A kind old lady with a croquet mallet could have saved Jones two strokes." Because Jones was an amateur, Diegel and Smith split the winner's check.

With the win, Jones matched John Ball's 40-year-old record of taking out the British Open and British Amateur championships in the same year. A measure of his exhaustion was that Jones accidentally left his clubs in the Savoy Hotel in London as he left for his ship, the *Europa*, in Southampton. The clubs followed him on another ship, the *Aquitania*, the next day. Back in New York, Jones received a ticker tape parade down Broadway.

Twenty-two days later, Jones, the defending U.S. Open champion, arrived at the Interlachen course in Minneapolis to play against a top-class field that included Tommy Armour, Walter Hagen, Al Espinosa, Johnny Goodman, Macdonald Smith, and Al Watrous. The 150 participants had been whittled down from an extraordinary 1,200 entries. Every good golfer in America wanted to win the nation's championship.

The temperature on the tournament's first day was 107 degrees, a record high that would stand for decades. Jones opened with a 71 to tie for third behind Tommy Armour and Macdonald Smith, and level with Whiffy Cox. A second-round 73—which included his ball skimming safely across the pond in front of the green on the par-five ninth hole—put him tied for second, two shots behind Horton Smith.

Despite bogeys on the last two holes of his third round, Jones's 68—a course record by two shots—had him leading the tournament by five. He struggled during the final round, including losing a ball on the seventeenth, but his 75 (for a four-round total of 287) was good enough to win by two shots over Macdonald Smith.

Jones tipped caddie Donovan Dale $85, somewhat more than the average per-round fee of $1. In addition to winning another U.S. Open, Jones had set a startling record—for eight of his last nine U.S. Opens, he had finished either first or second. He had also lost nearly 17 pounds over the three-day championship.

In late September, Jones arrived at Merion Golf Club in Pennsylvania to face some stiff competition in the U.S. Amateur, including Francis Ouimet, George von Elm, Jess Sweetser, Johnny Goodman—who so famously beat Jones in the first round of the tournament the previous year—and

George Voigt. The winner would be the player who showed the greatest resilience, patience, and poise.

Needless to say, interest in the tournament was at fever pitch. One hundred and fifty reporters descended on the club, and an army of Marines was employed to keep the crowd at bay. Jones shot 69 for his first qualifying round, and a second round 72 tied him for the lowest qualifying score for the Amateur, matching one of his own previous efforts. The field was reduced from 168 to 32 for the match-play finals.

Jones was not challenged in either of his first two matches, accounting for 27-year-old Ross Sommerville—winner of three Canadian Amateur titles—5 and 4 in the morning, and Fred Hoblitzer by the same comfortable margin in the afternoon. In the third round, the 36-hole quarterfinal, he beat the reigning Southern Californian champion, Fay Coleman, 5 and 4.

In the semifinal, he was up against his old pal Jess Sweetser, who once beat Jones 8 and 7 at Brookline. Jones, who had a reputation for never losing to the same person twice, was 4 up at lunch and closed out the match, 9 and 8.

In the final, he met 22-year-old former Princeton champ Eugene Homans from Englewood, New Jersey. Homans battled nerves and an even-par 72 in the morning from Jones, which had the champion 7 up at lunch. The match was all over on the eleventh hole of the afternoon round, Jones winning, 8 and 7.

Jones had won the Grand Slam. Fifty Marines protected him from 18,000 delirious fans, who wanted to congratulate Jones personally—many of them had just witnessed golf for the first time. The applause did not stop for five minutes.

Dressed in immaculate white pants, two-tone shoes, a dark jacket, and crisp white shirt and tie, Jones was presented the trophy by Findlay Douglas, president of the USGA. Jones handed $150 to his caddie, Howard Rexford, who had drawn Jones's name from a hat at the start of the tournament. Famously, Rexford kept Jones's ball for 30 years, then inexplicably used it in a match and lost it.

Jones's win made the front page of newspapers across the United States. He was hailed as a hero, one who played the sport in the right spirit, with the right level of competitiveness and a clear and uncompromising love of the game and respect for the rules. Two months later, he left golf as one of its great champions.

Character

...............•...............

Golf won't necessarily build character, but it will
always reveal character.

THOMAS FRIEDMAN, *CLASSIC SHOTS*

Golf camaraderie, like that of astronauts and Antarctic explorers,
is based on a common experience of transcendence; fat or thin,
scratch or duffer, we have been somewhere together
where nongolfers never go.

JOHN UPDIKE

Everyone said that Australian Greg Norman had a game that would, eventually, win The Masters. Possibly two or three of them. Booming drives, imagination, and a deft short game represented the complete package for success at Augusta, and Norman—the blond giant from Queensland—had each of these in bucketloads, plus a fearlessness and confidence that other golfers envied. Success followed him. During the 1980s and early 1990s, Norman spent 331 weeks as the number-one-ranked golfer in the world.

Norman came to the 1996 Masters having played there 15 times for seven top-ten finishes, including two seconds, two thirds, and a fourth. His two seconds had been in 1986, when he bogeyed the final hole to lose to Jack Nicklaus by a stroke; and in 1987, when Larry Mize chipped in from off the green on the eleventh for an improbable birdie to win the sudden-death play-off.

From the first round, when Norman shot a sizzling 63, which tied the course record, it appeared that 1996 would be his year of redemption. Subsequent rounds of 69 and 71 gave him a six-shot lead over Britain's Nick Faldo with a round to go. No one with such a lead had ever lost The Masters. Added to this, Faldo was up to his neck in a $12 million divorce. Faldo himself was so sure that Norman would win that he was late for practice for the final round.

The only question mark was that Norman had led majors seven times with a round to go and had recorded only one win—the 1986 British Open at Turnberry.

From the start of the final round, things didn't go right. Norman hooked his drive into the trees at the first hole and made a bogey and followed it with another bogey on the fourth. Then, after the first eight holes, Norman fell into an abyss. He bogeyed the ninth, tenth, and eleventh, by which time his lead had evaporated. He hit into the water on the twelfth for a double bogey, his fifth straight five.

On the fifteenth, his chip for an eagle missed by inches and he fell to the ground, as if shot. By the time he hit into the water again on the sixteenth for another double bogey, his humiliation was complete. Norman had missed 10 out of 18 greens and shot 78, 15 shots worse than his opening round.

As Faldo made a meaningless 16-foot birdie putt on the last hole, his 67 being enough to win by five shots, he didn't know how to react. There were no histrionics or fist pumping, just a deep breath and an almost resigned raising of the arms.

Norman approached him, a gigantic smile on his face, and

they hugged long and hard. Faldo later said he had whispered to Norman, "I don't know what to say. I just want to give you a hug. I feel horrible about what happened. I'm so sorry." As they walked off the green, arm in arm, Norman touched his cap to the crowd.

Norman later told a press conference, again with a broad and brave grin:

> I screwed up, but it's not the end of the world for me. My life is going to continue. I let this one get away, but I still have a pretty good life. I'll wake up tomorrow, still breathing, I hope. All these hiccups I have, they must be for a reason. All this is just a test. I just don't know what the test is yet.

Norman received thousands of cards and letters because of the dignity he showed in the face of crushing disappointment. Norman von Nida, the great Australian golfer and coach, and one of Norman's mentors, wrote: "The sportsmanship displayed by Norman and Faldo on the eighteenth green was one of the most memorable scenes in the history of the game. I was so proud of both men for showing the world the true spirit of the game, which I believe is competition and friendship."

Friendship

.... ● ....

I am quite certain that there has never been a greater addition to the lighter side of civilization than that supplied by the game of golf.

LORD BALFOUR

My worst day on the golf course still beats my best day in the office.

JOHN HALLISEY, *MONTEREY PENINSULA HERALD*, 1984

In 1949, a tall American golfer, Bill Campbell, arrived at Shannon Airport in southwest Ireland, en route to the British Amateur at Portmarnock. As he was changing money at the airport, the 26-year-old struck up a conversation with the bank manager, who asked him how long he had until his connecting flight to Dublin. When Campbell told him that he had three hours, the bank manager drew the blind, closed the bank, and phoned the Ennis Golf Club to say they would be on the first tee in fifteen minutes. They played nine holes before returning to the airport as firm friends. Thirty-nine years later, Campbell returned to Ireland for Cork Golf Club's centenary. The same banker, now retired and living in Galway, came out to watch him play. Campbell, who died in August 2013, told Adam Schupak from *Golfweek* magazine of the friendship, "This could only happen in golf."

That it happened to Campbell is perhaps not surprising. The West Virginian was universally loved for his generosity of spirit, his friendliness, and his adherence to the finest ideals of honesty and amateurism.

Campbell had a glittering amateur career, which included 32 tournament wins. Between 1951 and 1975, he played on eight Walker Cup teams, captaining the victorious 1955 team, which trounced the British team, 10–2, at St. Andrews. He was runner-up in the 1954 British Amateur and three times runner-up in the Canadian Amateur. He won three West Virginia Opens, four North and South Amateurs, and 15 West Virginia Amateur titles. He won the U.S. Senior Amateur in 1979 and 1980 and finished second in the 1980 U.S. Senior Open. He played in 14 U.S. Opens and 17 Masters.

His never-say-die attempts at America's greatest amateur event, the U.S. Amateur, won him much acclaim. He first played in the event in 1938, as a 15-year-old ("I topped the ball off the tee," he told Schupak. "There was a big storm, and I didn't have a towel, umbrella, or an extra golf glove"). He would play in it another 36 times. But success eluded him. "It had become a quest after the Holy Grail for me," he said of his attempts.

Finally, in 1964, aged forty-one and with a new set of custom-made irons, Campbell reached the final of the event at the Canterbury Country Club in Ohio. His opponent was Ed Tutwiler, who had beaten Campbell six of the seven times they had played in the final of the West Virginia Amateur. Campbell admitted he wasn't particularly confident. "How would you feel if you finally got to the final and had to play the guy who made a living out of beating you?" he said.

Campbell took the lead for the first and only time by winning the 35th hole, before halving the last to win 1-up. "I can't call it a noble victory, but it made up for a lot," he said.

In addition to spending three years in the West Virginia Legislature, Campbell twice served on the Executive Committee of the USGA (1962–1965 and 1977–1984). He was president in 1982 and 1983. In 1987, he was named Captain of the Royal and Ancient Golf Club of St. Andrews—the third American to hold that post—and became the first person to head both of golf's main governing bodies.

In 1956, Campbell was awarded the Bob Jones Award, the USGA's highest honor.

"In golf," Campbell was fond of saying, "there are no strangers, only friends you have never met."

Turning the Tide

...............●...............

You have to work hard to be on the top.
You have to wait for your moment.

It's been a tough fight, but there can only be one winner.
This time, it's me.

When Costantino Rocca—the burly golfer from Bergamo in
northern Italy—holed an improbable 49-foot putt for birdie

after fluffing a chip into the Valley of Sin on the seventy-second hole at the 1995 Open Championship at St. Andrews, forcing a four-hole playoff with American John Daly, the roar around the eighteenth green reverberated around the ancient Kingdom of Fife.

Rocca emitted a primeval scream as he fell to his knees and raised his fists to the heavens, before collapsing to the ground and punching the turf with delight. Daly, who finished his round earlier, stood stony-faced, before turning to walk to the practice green.

More than 1,200 miles away, two young brothers—Eduardo and Francesco Molinari—were watching the drama unfold on television on the outskirts of Turin. When Rocca's putt dropped, they jumped in the air and whirled around like dervishes, hugging each other. Surely, they reasoned, this was a sign; the 124-year wait for an Italian winner of the Open had come.

An hour later, the two boys were in tears. Rocca had lost the playoff by four shots, bogeying the first hole and then having a disastrous triple bogey on the third playoff hole, the infamous seventeenth on the Old Course, the Road Hole. The fact that he birdied the final playoff hole was no consolation; the wait for an Italian winner of the Open would have to continue.

Many Italians have tried to win the Open Championship. Some of Italian heritage have achieved it, including the great Gene Sarazen—born Eugenio Saraceni in Harrison, New York, the son of poor Sicilian immigrants—who won in 1932 at the Prince's Course in Kent, and Mark Calcavecchia (whose Italian surname translates to "old crowd"), who won the Open Championship at Royal Troon in 1989. Toney Penna, who was born in Naples but grew up in New York, came in third in the 1938 US Open at Cherry Hills and only played in one Open Championship, in 1954, where he made the cut.

And so, when people surveyed the draw at the 2018 Open Championship at Carnoustie, northeast of Dundee, searching for the likely winner, most would have skimmed over the name of world number 15, Francesco Molinari—the younger of the two brothers from Turin all those years ago, and the only Italian in the field. Sure, the 35-year-old was playing well, having won the BMW PGA Championship in May at Wentworth, holding off the Irishman Rory McIlroy by two shots and recording his maiden win in the USA, the Quicken Loans Classic in Maryland, shooting a final round 62 to win by eight shots in a zen-like performance.

But history doesn't lie—in 146 years of the Open Championship, the number of Italians who had won the event was, precisely, zero. Molinari's previous best finish was a tie for ninth in 2013.

The Italian arrived at Carnoustie on Monday, three days before the first round, to find a firm and fast layout, without much rough, but with strong winds predicted in the days ahead. He told the media Carnoustie was a "beast" that had beaten him up at the Dunhill Links Championship over the years. "I didn't particularly enjoy that feeling," he said. "It's a really tough course. You can try and play smart golf, but some shots you just have to hit it straight. There's no way around it. You can't really hide."

In his favor were recent unlikely winners in the event, including Henrik Stenson at Troon in 2016, the first Swede in history to lift the Claret Jug, and the unfancied Darren Clark from Northern Ireland, who won at Royal St. George's in 2011 after many in the press had said he was merely making up the numbers.

Molinari's first two rounds were workmanlike, 70 and 72 against par of 71, putting him six shots behind the leaders,

Americans Zach Johnson—who won two years earlier on the Old Course at St. Andrews—and Kevin Kisner.

In the third round, Molinari shot a bogey-free 65, which moved him up to outright fifth behind four Americans. Kisner, Xander Schauffele, and Jordan Spieth, who also shot a 65, led him by three, with Kevin Chappell one ahead. A shot behind Molinari were a bunch of big names including McIlroy, Tommy Fleetwood, Matt Kuchar, Webb Simpson, and three-time winner Tiger Woods, with whom Molinari would be paired in the final round. The interest in Woods, who was ranked 650th at the start of the year, was immense.

Kisner, Schauffele, and McIlroy all stumbled on the front nine in the final round in windy conditions, while Woods gathered birdies on the fourth and sixth holes to take the lead. Tiger-mania came to Carnoustie when word spread that Woods led the event he last won 12 years earlier. At the 11th, however, he hit his tee shot in the rough and his approach over the green. His chip shot came up short of the green, and he failed to get up-and-down, finishing with a double bogey. Another bogey at the 12th destroyed his chances.

Molinari, meanwhile, like ol' man river, kept rolling along. He began with 13 straight pars before a birdie at the 14th. Three more pars followed, and he stood on the 18th tee with a one-shot lead over Kisner and McIlroy. At the back of his mind surely were previous dramas on the same hole—Frenchman Jean van de Velde blowing a three-shot lead in 1999 before losing to Scotsman Paul Lawrie and, eight years later, Irishman Padraig Harrington and Spaniard Sergio Garcia shooting double bogey and bogey, respectively, on the hole before Harrington won the four-hole playoff.

Molinari was having none of it. A laser-like drive left him with a short-iron approach, which he chipped to within six-and-a-half feet. The putt never looked like missing. The Italian had played 37 holes of the hardest course on the Open rotation in very challenging conditions without a bogey.

He won by two shots over Kisner, McIlroy, Schauffele, and England's Justin Rose, who also finished with a 69. Defending champion Spieth shot 76 to finish four behind. Of the eight players in the final four groups on Sunday, only Molinari finished under par.

Molinari had to cancel his 9 p.m. flight home—not a hardship when you have just won $1.89 million—and told the media he had a sense of disbelief at being the first Italian to win not just the Open championship, but any Major championship.

"To go the weekend bogey-free, it's unthinkable," he said. "Playing with Tiger was another challenge. But I felt really good this morning. I felt I was ready for the challenge.

"To look at the names on that Claret Jug, they are the best golfers in history. For someone like me coming from Italy, not really a major golfing country, it's been an incredible journey. If Ferrari won today, they will get the headlines, but hopefully there were a lot of young kids watching on TV today, like I was watching Costantino back in 1995. Everyone knows he is my hero, and this win is for him as well as for me. Hopefully the kids watching will get as inspired as I was at the time."

Said Rocca, simply, "It was a grand demonstration of strength of character and concentration."

Helpfulness

...........•...........

I am the suggestion book.

J.F. ABERCROMBY, SECRETARY AT THE ADDINGTON GOLF CLUB,

TO A NEW MEMBER WHO ASKED FOR THE SUGGESTION BOOK

That the water in the bunkers on the 13th be changed.

SUGGESTION BOOK ENTRY BY LORD BRABAZON OF TARA

The golf club suggestion book is far more than a collection of advice from members to the committees and managers of their clubs, or the opportunity for members to vent their spleen at issues of food, course, or staff. It is, in many instances, as much a source of great humor as it is a reflection of long-term social change.

Here is a selection of entries from the suggestion books of various British golf clubs, accompanied in some instances by the response from the committee:

Since the water in the bunker at the 11th hole is apparently to be a permanent feature, the committee consider stocking it with trout.

Prestwick, 1975

.............•.............

That the rabbit catcher on the links be stopped carrying a gun in any circumstances near the course. He again pointed his gun at three members teeing off on the 16th today from a distance of 40 or 50 yards.

Rabbit catcher? What were the members' handicaps please?

Seacroft Golf Club

.............•.............

That some method of distinguishing the greens from the fairway be devised.

Wilmslow Golf Club

Could the clubhouse be moved a little more to the left please?

Rye, 1970

..............●..............

That the cockroaches be dealt with.

Formby, 1913

..............●..............

That the suggestion book be attended to and the suggestions answered.

This suggestion is considered frivolous.

Royal Ashdown Forest, 1934

..............●..............

On revisiting the Club I am glad to find that my suggestion of 23 Sept 1894 has received attention.

Woking, 1930

..............●..............

Mirror mirror on the wall,

The ground floor room has none at all,

For those of us who still have hair,

Please find a man to fix it there.

Ranfurly Castle

.............•.............

That better weather be provided.

This has been attended to, temporarily.

Many thanks—kindly persevere.

Royal West Norfolk, 1910

.............•.............

It is now eight years since I joined the club. I am still without a key to my locker.

Porters Park, 1947

.............•.............

31 December 1977: I suggest that the incumbent committee resigns en masse.

2 January 1978: I withdraw the preceding without reservation and offer my apology to my committee.

Helensburgh

.............•.............

It is suggested that the Irish Stew should have a touch of onion about it.

Noted.

Royal Cinque Ports

.............●.............

May an alternative Turkish cigarette to Abdullahs be supplied. They are expensive and nasty. Might the Anglo-American Cigarette Company's Kremlin be given a trial? They are 9s a 100.

Littlestone, 1925

.............●.............

That the specific gravity of afternoon tea be doubled.

Royal Wimbledon

.............●.............

No Club stilton, females at every table.

Royal Wimbledon, 1968

.............●.............

I suggest that the man responsible for the so-called pin placements for today's medal competition must be the greatest sadist in the history of the game.

A conscious decision was taken by the Links Manager to choose the driest spot he could find following the more or less continuous rain on the previous two days. The Marquis de Sade does not appear on his family tree.

Royal Liverpool, 1991

.............•.............

That the Club become affiliated with the Amateur Athletic Association and that Cridlaw J.G. be entered in the hammer event.

Chislehurst, 1961

.............•.............

Would the Captain please clarify acceptable hair length at this Club?

Two club lengths, stroke and distance.

Royal Cinque Ports

.............•.............

That the Committee pronounce publicly and categorically the purpose of the beautiful little trees planted behind the 3rd and 5th greens.

To grow into bigger trees.

Aldeburgh

Believing in Miracles

...............●...............

He was a pretty decent player until the day when,
for one brief shining moment, he was perfect.

SPORTS ILLUSTRATED, JANUARY 17, 1972

I aim at the hole.

1959 MASTERS CHAMPION ART WALL, WHEN ASKED HOW HE HAD
RECORDED 42 HOLES IN ONE

If it wasn't witnessed by four men of sound mind who had
nothing to gain by the story, surely no one would have believed

it. In any event, it was so outrageous no one could have dreamt it.

On a mild November afternoon in 1971 at the Brookwood Country Club in suburban Chicago, 22-year-old Assistant Professional Tom Doty holed, in four consecutive holes, a three-wood, a driver, a four-wood, and a nine-iron. His scores on those holes were two, one, one, two—an albatross (double eagle), back-to-back holes in one (one of which was another albatross), and an eagle.

Thankfully, he had witnesses: Manny Kantor, Peter Orofino, Harry Robbins, and Frank LaPuzza—four businessmen in their midfifties and midsixties, and longtime golfers whom Doty had joined on the first tee for a five ball.

Doty finished with a round of 59, thirteen under par. But his final score was almost forgotten against his miraculous four-hole stretch, which he played in ten under par. He played, for one magnificent hour, the best golf that had ever been played.

Single-mindedness

On most of the holes, just a pretty good shot is of no use at all.

GEORGE CRUMP, ON PINE VALLEY

George A. Crump has written his own eulogy, not in words
but in deeds. Whatever he has undertaken to do,
he has well and faithfully done.

SIMON CARR

In the first decade of the twentieth century, a larger-than-life Philadelphia hotelier—and fine golfer—George Crump decided he would build America's most spectacular and difficult golf course, one to test the best players in the country and, possibly, to produce a U.S. Amateur champion.

For many years, the colonial game of cricket had been the pastime of choice among high society in the Philadelphia region, and upward of 120 cricket clubs existed. But golf was on the rise.

Crump looked beyond the city for suitable land and came across what he considered the perfect site: next to a railway track in the rolling and remote Pine Barrens area of South Jersey, east of Philadelphia across the Delaware River. Course designer A.W. Tillinghast liked telling people that Crump spotted the land from a speeding train on the way to Atlantic City.

After inspecting the land, Crump said to his friend, two-time Philadelphia Amateur Champion Howard Perrin, "If you take care of the organization, I will build the golf course." Crump told his friends, simply, "I think we have happened on something pretty fine."

Crump bought the land—184 acres—for $8,750 in October 1912, and the first tree fell four months later. Tens of thousands of trees were cleared, streams were dammed to make lakes, and greens and fairways were fashioned. Importantly, an artesian well was sunk to 230 feet and a pumping station constructed to carry water to every part of the course.

The first five fairways were seeded in September 1913 and were ceremoniously opened in early November of the same year. Those present were aware that they were witnessing something special. Extraordinarily, the first eleven holes were completed within nineteen months.

For the first few months, Crump camped on the course—poring over plans by firelight—before he moved into a bungalow he built beside the fifth tee. He strode the grounds while the massive clearing campaign progressed, club in hand, playing shots to imaginary greens.

Although he had strong beliefs in the ideal routing for his course, Crump was also happy to receive advice. He hosted the best architects in the world including Tillinghast, Harry Colt from Sunningdale, Hugh Wilson, and Walter Travis. He listened intently to their suggestions, but there was never any doubt who was in charge.

The land that had driven away many others who had

tried to cultivate it would not spare Crump. The mud that had been dug from the streams and spread on the fairways as fertilizer actually impeded their growth, while chickweed, crabgrass, goosegrass, pearlwort, and brown spot created further problems. A drought hit, and World War I arrived, with its associated financial stresses.

Extraordinarily, the full eighteen-hole routing would take another six years to complete.

In January 1918, Crump—aged only forty-six—used a hunting shotgun to take his own life. Pine Valley historian Andrew Mutch writes, "It is surmised that the failing condition and unfinished state of the course, along with his bleak financial situation, led to his despondent condition." Eleven years earlier, Crump's wife, Belle, had died while on a tour of New England with friends, collapsing on a ferry between Manhattan and Jersey City. For years, Crump confided in friends that he missed her terribly.

Despite Crump's death, his family remained linked to the club, his sister Helen relieving the club of much of the debt that was owed to her brother. Around the same time, retired textile merchant and club member Grinnell Willis gave $20,000 for the completion of the course. By the summer of 1920, the full eighteen holes were completed. At the time, annual dues were $40, greens fees were $2.50 on weekdays and $5 on weekends, entrance fees were $200, and a room in the dormitory cost $3.50.

Crump's creation attracted huge praise. Architect Donald Ross said, "This is the finest golf course in America." Victor East described Pine Valley as "the best golf course I have ever seen." English golf writer Henry Longhurst said, "I look on it as the greatest of all inland courses, the perfect examination of the golfer's physical and psychological powers."

Today, Pine Valley—with its manicured fairways, vast sandy areas, glorious vistas, fast and hard greens, and often diabolical bunkers—is regularly voted the world's best, and toughest, course. The golfer stands on the first tee knowing that one false stroke could be the ruin of his round.

Although, tragically, Crump never saw the course completed, there is no doubt that he was the driving force behind its vision and construction. The Walker Cup was played at the club in 1936, and, today, the country's best golfers play each year for the Crump Cup.

"Pine Valley arose from the passion and commitment of one man. Without him the course would not exist," Mutch writes in his book *Crump's Dream*. "He recognized a specific need in the Philadelphia golf scene that he pursued with singular drive and focus."

In Pine Valley's clubhouse, there is a mural of the course's layout, painted in 1929 by Canadian Benjamin Kilvert. The mural carries words borrowed from Sir Christopher Wren's tomb in London's St. Paul's Cathedral—*Si monumentum requiris, circumspice*.

"If you seek his monument—look around you."

Sources and Further Reading

Alliss, Peter, *Peter Alliss's 100 Greatest Golfers*, Guild Publishing, London, 1989.

Alliss, Peter, *Supreme Champions of Golf*, Willow Books, London, 1986.

Armour, Tommy, *Tommy Armour's ABCs of Golf*, Simon & Schuster, New York, 1967.

Ballesteros, Severiano, and Doust, Dudley, *Seve: the Young Champion*, Hodder & Stoughton, 1982.

Barrett, Ted, *The Daily Telegraph Golf Chronicle*, Carlton Books Limited, London, 2005.

Blaine, Michael, *The King of Swings*, Houghton Mifflin Company, Boston, 2006.

Boswell, Thomas, *Strokes of Genius*, Simon & Schuster, London, 1987.

Brown, Cal, *Masters Memories*, Sleeping Bear Press, Ann Arbor, Michigan, 1998.

Clayton, Mike, *Golf from the Inside*, Scribe Publications, Melbourne, 2003.

Darwin, Bernard, *Darwin on the Green*, Souvenir Press, London, 1986.

Davis, Martin, *Ben Hogan: the Man Behind the Mystique*, American Golfer, Greenwich, Connecticut, 2002.

Demaret, Jimmy, *My Partner Ben Hogan*, Peter Davies, London, 1954.

de St. Jorre, John, *Legendary Golf Clubs of Scotland, England, Wales and Ireland*, Edgeworth Editions, Florida, 1999.

de St. Jorre, John, *Legendary Golf Clubs of the American East*, Edgeworth Editions, West Palm Beach, Florida, 2003.

Dobereiner, Peter (ed.), *The Golfers: The Inside Story*, Collins, London, 1982.

Dodson, James, *Ben Hogan: the Authorised Biography*, Aurum Press, London, 2004.

Ferguson, Duncan, and Wilson, John, *The Golf Club Suggestion Book*, Tempus Publishing, Gloucestershire, 2006.

255

Finegan, James W., *Where Golf Is Great*, Artisan, New York, New York, 2006.

Frost, Mark, *The Grand Slam*, Time Warner Books, London, 2004.

Frost, Mark, *The Greatest Game Ever Played,* Hyperion Books, New York, 2002.

Frost, Mark, *The Match: the Day the Game of Golf Changed Forever,* Hyperion, New York, New York, 2007.

Garrity, John, "Open and Shut," *Sports Illustrated*, June 2006.

Gleason, Dan, *The Great, the Grand and the Also-Ran*, Random House, New York, New York, 1976.

Gregory, Paul, *Greatest Moments in Golf*, Exeter Books, New York, New York, 1987.

Harmon Jr., Claude "Butch," *The Pro: Lessons About Golf and Life from My Father Claude Harmon Sr.*, Three Rivers Press, New York, New York, 2007.

Hill, Dave, and Seitz, Nick, *Teed Off*, Prentice Hall, Upper Saddle River, New Jersey, 1977.

Jacobs, John, and Newell, Steve, *50 Years of Golfing Wisdom*, HarperCollins, New York, New York, 2006.

Jenkins, Dan, *Dead Solid Perfect*, Doubleday, New York, New York, 2000

Jenkins, Dan, *The Dogged Victims of Inexorable Fate*, Simon & Schuster, New York, New York, 1990.

Jones, Robert Tyre, *Bobby Jones on Golf*, Broadway Books, New York, New York, 1992.

Longhurst, Henry, *Round in Sixty-eight*, W. Laurie, London, 1953.

Longhurst, Henry, *The Best of Henry Longhurst*, Golf Digest, New York, New York, 1978.

McCord, Robert (ed.), *The Quotable Golfer*, The Lyons Press, New York, New York, 2000.

McDonnell, Michael, *The Complete Book of Golf*, The Kingswood Press, Tadworth, 1985.

MacKenzie, Alister, *Golf Architecture*, Simpkin, Marshall, Hamilton, Kent & Co Ltd, London, 1982

MacKenzie, Alister, *The Spirit of St. Andrews*, Broadway Books, New York, New York, 1998.

Mackintosh, David (ed.), *Golf's Greatest Eighteen*, Contemporary Books, New York, New York, 2003.

Mutch, Dr. Andrew, *Crump's Dream: The Making of Pine Valley, 1913–1936,* Pine Valley Golf Club, Pine Valley, New Jersey, 2013.

Nelson, Byron, *How I Played the Game*, Taylor Trade Publishing, Texas, 1993.

Nicklaus, Jack, with Bowden, Ken, *My Story*, Ebury, London, 1997.

Parkes, Marty (ed.), *Classic Shots*, National Geographic, Washington, 2007.

Player, Gary, *Grand Slam Golf*, Cassell & Co., London, 1967.

Resnick, J.P. (ed.), *The Little Treasury of Golf*, Black Dog & Leventhal Publishers, New York, New York, 1996.

Rice, Grantland, *The Tumult and the Shouting*, Barnes, New York, New York, 1954.

Rubenstein, Lorne, and Neuman, Jeff, *A Disorderly Compendium of Golf*, Workman, New York, New York, 2006.

Sarazen, Gene, with Wind, Herbert Warren, *Thirty Years of Championship Golf*, Prentice-Hall, New York, New York, 1950.

Shackleford, Geoff, *Alister MacKenzie's Cypress Point Club*, Sleeping Bear Press, Ann Arbor, Michigan, 2000.

Sidorsky, Robert (ed.), *Golf's Greatest Moments*, H.N. Abrams, New York, New York, 2003.

Simpson, Sir Walter, *The Art of Golf*, Oleander Press, Cambridge, 2008.

Snead, Sam, *Sam Snead's How to Play Golf,* Garden City Publishing, New York, New York, 1946.

Snead, Sam, with Stump, Al, *The Education of a Golfer*, Cassell & Co., London, 1962.

Sommers, Robert, *Golf Anecdotes*, Oxford University Press, Oxford, 1996.

Sullivan, Pat, and Chieger, Bob, *The Book of Golf Quotations*, Stanley Paul & Co., London, 1987.

Thomson, Peter, with Perkin, Steve, *Lessons I Have Learned,* Geoff Slattery Publishing, Melbourne, 2005.

Trevino, Lee, and Blair, Sam, *They Call Me Super Mex*, Random House, New York, New York, 1982.

Venturi, Ken, *Getting Up and Down*: *My Sixty Years in Golf*, Triumph Books, Chicago, Illinois, 2004.

Von Nida, Norman, and Robertson, Ben, *The Von: Stories and Suggestions from Australian Golf's Little Master*, University of Queensland Press, Brisbane, 1999.

Ward-Thomas, Pat, et al., *The World Atlas of Golf*, Colporteur Press, Sydney, 1984.

Williams, Michael, *Grand Slam: Golf's Major Championships*, Viscount Books, London, 1988.

Acknowledgments

The author would especially like to thank Emma Allen, and Archie, Max, Zoe, and Matilda Allen. Thanks also to Pilar Aguilera, Chris Atkinson, Charlie Baillieu, Kimbal Baker, Michael Barrowcliffe, Olivia Blake, Ross Bradfield, Eric Brodie, Fabian Burgess, Alf Cattanach, Charles Churchill, Mike Clayton, Jane Cotter, Jim Davis, Tom Doak, Ed Ervasti, John Fawcett, Anne Findlay, Chris Haslam, Richard Hatt, Monica Haynes, Sally Heath, Terri King, Helen Koehne, Foong Ling Kong, Chris Leach, David Lowe, Eric Lucas, Matt McKenna, Tim Morris, Andrew Mutch, Andrew Newbold, Tracy O'Shaughnessy, Paul Rak, Charley Raudenbush, Mignonne Rawson, Bill Shean, Tom Smiley, Paul Smitz, Peter Stackpole, Peter Thomson, Brian Twite, Andrew Wallis, and Craig Williams.

The Publisher would like to thank Little, Brown Book Group for permission to reproduce material from Mark Frost's *The Greatest Game Ever Played*.